Dieter Seibert

Eastern Alps
The Classic Routes
on the Highest Peaks

Edited from an original translation by Jill Neate

Diadem Books · London

Cover photograph: Nearing the top of the Wildspitze
Photo: Sepp Brandl
Half Title: An engraving of the North Face of Cima Presanella
Frontispiece: The Biancograt on Piz Bernina.

Picture credits (page numbers): G. Achberger 48/49;
H. Bauregger 86 (bottom); S. Garnweidner 83 (top and bottom),
87 (top), 90 bottom, 91 (top), 155; L. Gensetter 31; W. Heiss 39;
R. Lindel 45; K. Puntschuh 84 (bottom); W. Rauschel 2, 86 top, 88, 96;
E. Reismüller 63, 109, 148; B. Ritschel 95 top; H. Wagner 56,
120/121, 165; F. Zengerle 71, 84 (top), 85, 91 (bottom),
94 (top), 92/93, 113, 115, 124/125, 133, 135, 139, 151;
all others by Dieter Seibert.

Sketch maps by Dieter Seibert.

British Library Cataloguing in Publication Data:
Seibert, Dieter
    Eastern Alps: Classic Routes on the
    Highest Peaks
    I. Title
    798.522094947

ISBN 0-906371-54-6

German edition ©1990 Verlag J. Berg,
in the Sudwest Verlag GmbH & Co KG, Munich.
English translation © 1992 Diadem Books.

Printed in Germany

Contents

Contents

The Most Beautiful Objectives

The Fascination of Glacier Routes

The German edition of this guide is called *Glacier Peaks of the Eastern Alps* as it is glaciers which give mountains that added degree of stature and interest. No matter how wild and imposing a rock peak may be, it is the ice-covered peaks which radiate the greatest fascination. The great number of alpinists who love these glacier excursions are, so to speak, a 'many-footed' proof of this, thus this guide is solely concerned with expeditions that have a significant glacier component.

The Eastern Alps have mountains of a moderate scale when compared to the Western Alpine giants but because many are heavily glaciated they preserve a real aura of challenge and beauty. Yet the route descriptions, not only in German, but also in English are scattered through numerous guidebooks and the time is long overdue to present a selection of the best expeditions in one volume. Many well-known and popular peaks are described, together with a number that are less well-known. Almost without exception the ascents described follow the easiest and often the original routes up these big peaks. They should be well within the scope of any experienced glacier traveller and of course a number of the climbs can be extended by adding interesting traverses to convenient peaks.

Conditions

Almost all the peaks described here are steeper at the top than lower down and with heights of well over 3000m, the difficulties are very dependent on the prevailing conditions. Fresh snow on the rocks, hard old snow or even bare ice can quickly change an easy route into a dangerous one. The summit ridge of the Wildspitze is one example, for the most part an easy snow trudge, can at certain times become a very precarious ice ridge.

Wind is another factor to take into account as it often sculpts summit ridges into dangerous cornices or knife-edges. Thus the final ridge of Similaun may be a broad snow ridge on one occasion and a precarious ice arête another time. Climbers should also be aware of the still serious danger of avalanches in summertime after new snow or a mild night.

Glaciers

Climber dies in crevasse fall! Many alpinists don't take this danger very seriously, as their reckless behaviour shows. All glacier routes presuppose four conditions:

● Full equipment. That means, amongst other things, an ice axe for each person, crampons, sufficient rope, spare line and a sit harness.

● Mastery of crevasse rescue. This must be practised in circumstances corresponding to a serious fall. Practice on rock and open crevasses is only half the story. It is completely incomprehensible that many mountaineering courses are content with this sort of dry run. Once the ice is covered with snow it gives rise to all sorts of problems.

● The fullest concentration whilst on the glacier – tight rope between climbers reduces the length of any fall and the likelihood of others being dragged after.

● A good knowledge of glaciers – those who understand how fractures develop and can recognize the direction of individual crevasses, can lay a much safer trail. Moreover, the possibility of a fall into a crevasse depends a great deal on the prevailing conditions. In soaking wet snow it is much increased! After a mild night, no one with any sense will set out on a route over a glacier full of crevasses. There are always less dangerous objectives near each hut. Most hut wardens will gladly advise which route is suitable for the prevailing conditions.

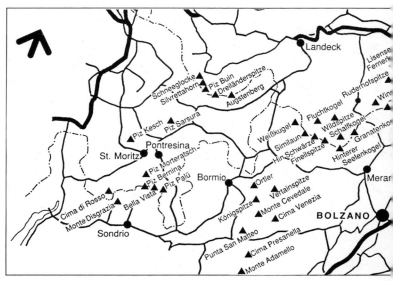

Huts

An overnight stop is necessary for almost all the big peaks in this guidebook. Almost all of the huts mentioned belong to the Alpine Clubs of Switzerland, Germany, Austria and Italy; so one should be a member of one of them (or another National organisation enjoying reciprocal rights). In the height of summer many huts are packed to overflowing, especially at weekends so a previous booking can secure a place to sleep.

Timings

All estimates of the time a climb takes can only be comparative figures. This is doubly true for snow routes. In this guidebook, the times are based on good conditions, the existence of a proper track, a light rucksack (i.e. for a day trip) and for climbers well able to cope with the difficulties involved.

Gradings

The conventional alpine French grades have been introduced to the English language edition in an attempt to create some correlation between the climbs. This can be complicated by the scale of routes – high and long climbs, however technically easy, always have an added degree of seriousness. Also a set of tracks across a crevassed glacier greatly simplifies route-finding and reduces anxiety. Finally poor visibility can make some routes infinitely more difficult.

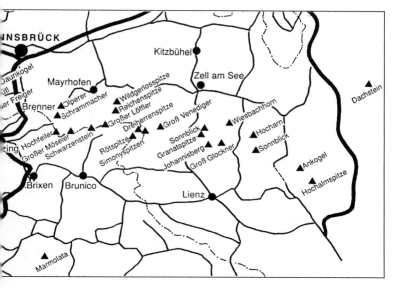

Silvretta Group

In something of a record for the Eastern Alps, the highest summit above the 3km broad and 700m high Jamtal Glacier is the Dreiländerspitze at the modest height of 3197m. The position of the Silvretta gives rise to unusually heavy glaciation, as the Vorarlberg section to the north-west is subject to especially high snowfall. To some extent the rain clouds spill over the weather divide which runs approximately along the crest west of the Jamtal but the end result is that the mountains west of the Jamtal have bigger glaciers than those to the east. The southern slopes of the Silvretta facing the Lower Engadine lie in the rain shadow, causing Piz Minschun (3068m) to be completely free of ice. In this connection, it is also striking that in high summer one can climb both the principal peaks in the group, Piz Linard (3411m) and the Fluchthörner (3399m) without coming into contact with any ice. For this reason, these peaks are excluded from this guidebook.

The Silvretta gets its special magic from the contrast between the gleaming white of its glaciers and its mostly dark coloured rocks. Moreover, in many cases the rock emerges very abruptly and steeply from the ice, rising in long ridges, which bristle with numerous pinnacles and towers. Thus here too there are also obvious rock-climbing peaks, like the Verstanklahorn and, above all, the black obelisk of the Grosslitzner. The well-known glacier peaks, such as Piz Buin and the Dreiländerspitze, are also striking in form but nevertheless present no particular climbing problems. With few exceptions, the routes over the glaciers range from flat to moderately steep. However, there are plenty of dangerous crevasse zones, so watch your step!

Also worthy of note is the very beautiful glacier country in the region of the Silvretta Haus, which is reached from Klosters in the Prättigau district via the Sardascatal. Here the Silvrettahorn, Piz Fliana (3281m) and the glacier crest are attractive objectives and the above mentioned Verstanklahorn (3298m) is one of the very demanding rock-climbing peaks.

View of the Silvrettahorn from the east. At the top (left of centre) is the Egghornlücke at the foot of the rock ridge; in the foreground is the Ochsentaler Glacier. ▷

Schneeglocke, 3223m
Silvrettahorn, 3244m

On the crest which separates the Ochsental from the Klostertal stands a whole row of decidedly beautiful and mostly rather rugged three thousanders. Only the most southerly peak, the Silvrettahorn (3244m) is frequently visited, whereas the Schattenspitze (3202m), a striking, almost black and rather unfriendly rock trihedral, is little frequented. Between the two rises the Schneeglocke (Snowbell) which, thanks to its glaciated North Face, really deserves its name. Nowadays the ice is melting away more and more and so by late summer the North-East Ridge is partly a rock arête.

The Schneeglocke has been selected because of its combination possibilities. You can climb it by its ordinary route or – much

more varied and also harder – make a little round trip out of the northern and ordinary routes. Moreover, the traverse to the Silvrettahorn involves only easy block climbing. Another possibility is to traverse the Silvrettahorn starting from the Wiesbadener Hut in the Ochsental and descending over the Schneeglocke and down to the Klostertal and the Bielerhöhe. By this route the southern ascent of the Silvrettahorn over the broken Ochsental Glacier provides the greatest difficulties.

First Ascent J. Jacot with Jegen and Schlegel, 1865.

Character and Demands PD– The western ascent of the Schneeglocke is easy, over a glacier with crevasses, and block climbing (I). The North Face is short but very steep (up to 45°. The traverse to the Silvrettahorn involves easy climbing (I). The southern ascent to the Silvrettahorn is over a broken glacier, with climbing up to II.

Timings Bielerhöhe to Schneeglocke 4½ hrs; Wiesbadener Hut to Silvrettahorn 3 hrs; from summit to summit 1 hr.

Best Map AV-Karte, 1:25,0000 Sheet 26 *Silvretta*; Swiss Landescarte, 1:50,000 Sheet 247 *Tarasp*.

Approach From the Vorarlberg side, go up the Montafon valley, then follow the twisting Silvretta alpine highway to Bielerhöhe (2036m, 45km from Bludenz). From the Tirol side, go up the Paznauntal to Galtur (1584m), continuing on the pass road (48km from Landeck). There are relatively inexpensive toll roads on both stretches.

Starting Point Bielerhöhe (2036m) which is on the Rhine/Danube watershed. There is a big reservoir right at the top of the pass (Silvretta Stausee). There are two hotels and lower down is the Madlener Haus (1968m, DAV, 100 beds, vehicle access). Parking on the east side of the lake.

Other Peaks From Bielerhöhe, the Hohes Rad (2934m, on a path 2¾ hrs) is a peak offering a celebrated view.

The Schneeglocke Ascent From Bielerhöhe, cross the dam wall and continue southwards along the western edge of the lake to the mouth of the Klostertal. Cross to the eastern side of the stream and walk up the valley on a broad path to the end of the flat part (2400m). Now turn off left and ascend the moraine fields south-eastwards to the arm of the Klostertal Glacier which descends from under the North Face of the Rotflue. Ascend the glacier (crevasses) to its topmost corner. Climb the block-cum-snow slope on to the South Ridge of the Schneeglocke and follow this easily to the summit.

Alternative approach by the North Face This is best

approached from the upper Klostertal and the northern arm of the Klostertal Glacier. Ascend the glacier as far as the notch between the Schattenspitze and the Schneeglocke. Now climb the beautiful and very steep snow slope to the summit.

Continuation to the Silvrettahorn Proceed as above as far as the South Ridge of the Schneeglocke and follow a block ridge over P.3190 to the summit (I).

Silvrettahorn from the Ochsental From the Wiesbadener Hut (see next chapter for approach details) climb up to the Ochsentaler Glacier, past the Grüne Kuppe (2579m), and ascend to and follow its western bank (many crevasses). Higher up traverse right across a snow basin into the most northerly dip in the Egghornlücke. Now, either climb mostly left of the South Ridge up its crumbly flank and approach the summit from the west (I); or – much nicer – ascend more or less on the ridge (II).

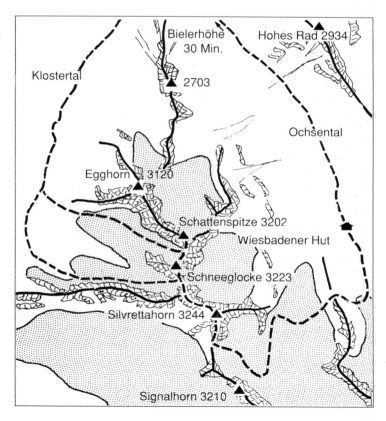

Piz Buin, 3312m

Although Piz Buin is 99m lower than the highest peak in the Silvretta Group, Piz Linard, it is more famous than all the other mountains in the area. The fact that there is no higher peak in the Vorarlberg may contribute to this. Moreover, its beautiful rock form dominates the valleys of the Ochsental to the north and Val Tuoi in the Lower Engadine. The crowd of visitors on fine summer and spring days is correspondingly great, especially since there are hardly any serious obstacles in good conditions. Nevertheless, there are always some climbers who have problems with Piz Buin. The popularity of the mountain means that it is often not taken seriously enough. At this height the northern sections can soon become iced and the exposed sections thus become much more tricky!

First Ascent J.A. Specht, J. Weilenmann with Pöll and Pfitscher, 1865.

Character and Demands F+ A route over medium-sized glaciers, some crevasse areas, a steeper summit block with a beaten path on scree, easy in good conditions (one section of I+), nevertheless often icy on account of its northern position.

Timings From Bielerhöhe to the hut 2 hrs; from there to the top 2¾ hrs.

Best Maps / Approach See p12.

Starting Point Bielerhöhe (2036m) on the watershed between the Rhine and the Danube. There is a big reservoir with two dams right at the top of the pass. There are two hotels and, to the west of and somewhat below the pass, the Madlener Haus (1968m, DAV, 100 beds ☎ 05558 8232, vehicle access). Parking on the eastern side of the lake.

Base Wiesbadener Hut (2443m, DAV Wiesbaden Section, 200 beds ☎ 05519 202), situated on the broad pastures high up the Ochsental, with a very beautiful mountain background; an excellent centre.

Other Peaks There is a relatively easy excursion up the Ochsenkopf (3057m, 1¾ hrs), or combined with the Tiroler Kopf (3103m, 1 hr from summit to summit), an extended itinerary offering attractive climbing at Grade II.

Hut Climb From Bielerhöhe, cross the eastern dam and follow the jeep track along the side of the lake to the hut. However,

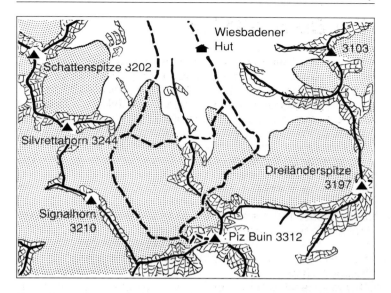

there is a nicer variation starting a third of the way along the lake, where a footpath branches off to the left. Follow this upwards across the slopes and above the jeep track continue up into the Ochsental to the hut. This route provides better views of the rugged Schattenspitze (3202m) and other points of interest.

Summit Climb From the hut, firstly ascend the valley on the upper path, then turn right on to the Vermunt Glacier, which is reached at a height of 2600m. Traverse the gentle ice slopes southwards, then ascend more steeply westwards (crevasses) towards the Wiesbadener Grätli. Climb a high, abrupt step to the left hand notch. On the other side of the notch, traverse the almost level upper basin of the Ochsentaler Glacier, contouring around the rock foot of Piz Buin to the Buinlücke (3054m). Follow the tracks up the steep, stony slope obliquely to the left to the blunt North-West Ridge. The rock step is climbed up a gully (the so-called Chimney), then ascend easier ground to the summit.

Descent Variant If you wish to return directly to Bielerhöhe after your ascent, you can descend the Ochsentaler Glacier, keeping close to its left hand side. In the middle section an extensive crevasse zone has to be crossed below which it is best to move across to P.2579 and down to the Wiesbadener Hut.

Dreiländerspitze, 3197m

The Dreiländerspitze is one of the best known and most climbed peaks in the western Austrian Alps, its strategic position above two much visited huts making it a tempting objective. The peak rises out of the broad and quite gentle ice slopes of the Vermunt Glacier like a bold black horn, supported by the typical pinnacled ridges of the Silvretta Group. Here the borders of Vorarlberg, Tirol and Graubünden meet. This fact is also reflected in the nomenclature, the ice streams on the three sides of the peak being described respectively as 'Gletscher', 'Ferner' and 'Vadret'.

Only the last 150 metres of the ascent offer any difficulty and here there is a steep snow slope and a rock ridge, the final metres of which are knife-edged and exposed. In good conditions they present no problems. Thus the ascent from the Wiesbadener Hut is a short, easy pleasure trip. The route from the Jamtal is more serious and exacting, adorned as it is with its eponymous glacier full of crevasses and icefalls. It also takes one and a half hours longer, but naturally that makes it more impressive!

The Dreiländerspitze from the north, showing the face ascended.

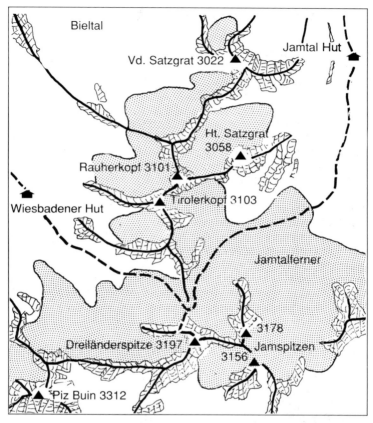

First Ascent T. Petersen, with O. Morell and D. Barbenda.
Character and Demands F+ Either an easy or an exacting
glacier route, with a short snow slope, rock ridge, and exposed
knife-edge finish (I).
Timings Wiesbadener Hut to summit 2½ hrs; from the Jamtal
Hut 4 hrs.
Best Maps See p12.

Approach Up the Paznauntal to Galtür (1584m), continuing
on the Silvretta alpine highway (toll road) to Bielerhöhe (see
p12). Or from Vorarlberg up the Montafon valley.
Valley Base Galtür (1584m), a popular holiday resort at the
mouth of the Jamtal in Paznaun; or Bielerhöhe (2036m, 2 hotels
and lower down the DAV Madlener Haus) on the top of the

pass dividing Tirol from Vorarlberg. Starting point for many excursions.

Bases Wiesbadener Hut (2443m), see p14; Jamtal Hut, see p19.

Hut Climbs See pp15/19.

The Vermunt Glacier Route From the Wiesbadener Hut, climb the highest track up the valley across the scree slopes and then continue uphill along the northern side of the Vermunt Glacier for a good distance. Now get on to the glacier near the ridge and traverse towards the striking snow triangle of the Dreiländerspitze. Ascend steeply from left to right on the always big track to a shoulder on the North-West Ridge. Climb easy rocky ground to the foresummit and a short rock knife-edge to the summit cross.

The Jamtal Glacier Route From the Jamtal Hut, ascend a distinct track to the snout of the Jamtal Glacier. Continue up the big basin on the western side of the glacier, then pass close to the rocks of the Ochsenkopf on account of crevasses. Keeping parallel to the ridge all the time, climb up to the Obere Ochsenscharte, where you meet the track coming up from the Wiesbadener Hut. Continue as above.

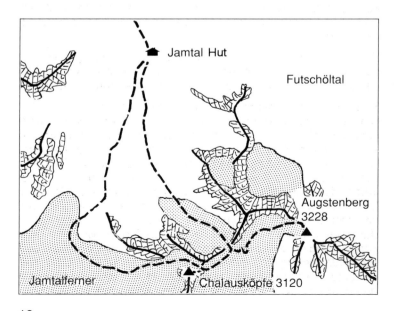

Augstenberg, 3228m

This well-known ski peak provides an attractive and varied summer excursion, but the Chalaus Glacier with its many crevasses poses a tricky problem. This leads to a surprising view from the notch (Fuorcla Chalaus), looking far to the south across many mountain chains as far as the Ortler. Finally there is the quite peculiar knife-edged snow ridge in the middle of the Vadret da Chalaus, which has to be overcome before one can reach this fairly high summit.

First Ascent J. Coaz, 1849
Character and Demands F+ Altogether not a difficult glacier route, although the numerous crevasses require care.
Timings Hut approaches 3 hrs and 1 hr; to the summit 3½ hrs.
Best Maps See p12.

Approach From Landeck or from Arlberg to the Paznauntal and then by a good road up the valley to Galtür.
Valley Base Galtür, popular holiday resort in the almost tree-less valley bottom; starting point for many excursions in the Silvretta and Verwall areas.
Base Jamtal Hut (2165m, DAV, Schwaben Stuttgart Section, 220 beds ☎ 05443 40814), situated on a ridgeback at the branching of the Jamtal, with an unusually rich choice of excursions.

Hut Climb From Galtür, follow the motor road up the flat-bottomed Jamtal to Scheibenalm (1838m, vehicle access this far up to 8am). Then continue along the little road to the hut.

Summit Climb Instead of taking the path to the Jamtal Glacier, ascend in the direction of the Steinmannli, then traverse obliquely up across the mostly rock-covered slopes and round a rock corner to the Chalaus Glacier. Traverse the narrow little crevassed glacier up into the Fuorcla Chalaus notch (3003m, the Swiss frontier). On the other side, cross the Vadret da Chalaus and a snow ridge into the upper basin, then climb the glacier slope and finally scree to the gap between the two summits. Turn left to gain the highest point.
Descent Variation From the Fuorcla Chalaus, continue south-wards along the ridge into the notch between the two Chalaus-köpfe (3120m, up the block ridge to the summit, II). Descend northwards, keeping on the right hand side of the Jamtal Glacier all the time (crevasses) to the path and so back to the hut.

Mountains of the Engadine

The Upper Engadine is one of the most beautiful spots in the Alps, with its kilometre-wide, flat valley bottoms, deep blue sheets of water and really big, elegant ice peaks everywhere. No wonder then that places like St. Moritz entice people – even princes and presidents – by the thousands. The majestic peaks too, first and foremost naturally Piz Bernina, the only four-thousander in the Eastern Alps, and the 'film star' peak Piz Palü, are powerful magnets. Yet even in the mighty Bernina group, with its enormous glaciers reminiscent of the Western Alps, apart from the few fashionable peaks, only a handful of people know the beautiful and not particularly difficult Piz Zupo (3996m); while other ice peaks like Piz Sella (3511m) and Piz Tremoggia (3441m) attract at best ski touring enthusiasts. For anyone interested there are thus many other attractive possibilities in the Bernina. The principal difficulties mainly consist of the very broken glaciers. For example, from the Coaz Hut one climbs Piz Glüschaint (3597m) up a veritable labyrinth of crevasses on the Vadret da Roseg.

In the Bregaglia Group to the south-west the glaciers are also rough and impressive. Here, however, they are often squeezed in between rock peaks that are smooth as walls. The 'young' granite contributes pinnacles and towers to their imposing appearance and excellent rock for climbing. Thus the Bregaglia is better known to the rock enthusiasts than to lovers of glaciers, though there are some good glacier approached peaks. Contrasting with these peaks are the nearby gentle, sedate gneiss mountains of the Albula Chain north-west of the main Engadine valley which, although about the same height, are substantially less glaciated. Yet in other districts Piz Kesch, Piz Vadret or Piz d'Err would definitely stand out from the rest; here, so close to the famous giants of the Upper Engadine, they are little regarded but offer more opportunity for peace and contemplation.

On the approach to the Boval Hut (Bernina). View from Chünetta of
the Morteratsch Glacier, Piz Palü and (right) Bella Vista. ▷

Piz Kesch, 3418m

Piz Kesch, highest peak in the Albula Group, rises far above its surroundings, with some really high faces on its almost kilometre-wide wall. Only to the north is there a biggish glacier, the Vadret Porchabella. Its rather concealed ramp runs high up the mountain and thus offers the easiest approach, for there is left a mere 150m of height gain to the top. This final rocky section has no great difficulties when the rock is dry, but becomes more dangerous when snow-covered; particularly if the snow is hard or icy. The route from the Engadine offers more variety than that from the Kesch Hut. Especially picturesque is the area near the Porta d'Es-cha, with its contrasting snow slopes and black rock pinnacles.

First Ascent J. Coaz, J. Reischer, C. Casper, J. Tscharner, 1846.
Character and Demands PD Short steep steps but only moderate glacier and snow with some crevasses; scree and block climbing (1) to the summit.
Timings From the Albula highway to the hut 1½ hrs; from there to the summit 2½ hrs.
Best Map Swiss Landeskarte, 1:50,000 Sheet 258 *Bergün*.

Approach Above La Punt in the Upper Engadine the twisting road continues over the Albula Pass (2312m) to Bergün. From La Punt go up the road, with its nine hairpins, to Punt Granda (2256m) 2km east of the top of the pass.

Valley Base La Punt (1697m), one of the many smaller towns in the broad valley on the fringe of the Upper Engadine.
Hut Base Es-cha Hut (2594m, SAC Bernina Section, 40 beds ☎ 08271 755) with a particularly beautiful open view to the Bernina Group.

Hut Climb From Punt Granda, make a rising traverse eastwards across the slopes to the Gualdauna saddle. Contour around the head of a small valley across vegetated slopes, then finally climb up the Es-cha Hut.
Summit Climb Ascend the ridge behind the hut for 200m, then turn left on to the broad moraines dotted with small lakes. After crossing the moraines, regain the ridge and turn right into a small snow basin. Climb a short step (snow or rock with a

steel cable) to the Porta d'Es-cha (3008m). On the other side of the col, descend slightly on to the flat Vadret da Porchabella and ascend it westwards to the right hand upper corner of the glacier. Climb steep snow, or just to the left of it, up to the North-East Ridge, then left again up gullies and over ledges and steps on the flank to the summit.

Descent Descend by the same route.

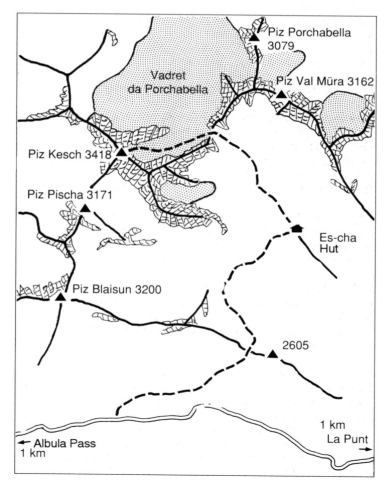

Piz Sarsura, 3178m

South of the Flüela Pass, which connects Davos and the Lower Engadine, is the tucked away Vadret group of the Albula. This is a mountain district with glaciers, snow peaks and the impressive, black pinnacle wall of Piz Vadret (Romansh for glacier peak). The hidden position of this clutch of peaks could explain why they are mainly frequented by the Swiss during the summer. Yet it is possible to climb them in one day from the Susasca valley. In relation to the height of the mountains, the amazingly heavy glaciation is due to the abundant snowfall for which Davos is well-known.

It is hard to pick one of the peaks. Piz Grialetsch (3131m), the 'backdoor' peak of the Grialetsch Hut, is reached quickest. Piz Sarsura shows itself as an impressive snow dome which can be easily traversed. More demanding is the black cockscomb ridge of Piz Vadret (3229m), whose ridges offer Grade III climbing. The safest and quickest route up this ridge is by the South Ridge and to reach it one must traverse the Fuorcla Vallorgia (3½ hrs from the Grialetsch Hut, III–, friable in places).

First Ascent Unknown

Character and Demands F A route over broad, mostly gentle glacier slopes, yet with some crevasses.

Timings Direct ascent from valley to summit 4 hrs; from the hut 2½ hrs; from valley to hut 2 hrs.

Best Maps Swiss Landeskarte, 1:50,000 Sheets 258 *Bergün* and 259 *Ofenpass*, or 1:25,000 Sheets 1217 *Scalettapass* and 1218 *Zernez*.

Approach To Susch in the Lower Engadine, then on the Flüela Pass road to Chant Sura (2150m); or from Davos over the Flüela Pass (2383m).

Starting Point Chant Sura (2150m), a small village about 3km east of the Flüela Pass.

Hut Base Grialetsch Hut (2542m, SAC St. Gallen Section, 66 beds ☎ 081 46 34 36), situated amidst the attractive, lake scenery of the Fuorcla da Grialetsch.

Other Peaks Piz Grialetsch (3131m) and Piz Vadret (3229m), described above.

Hut Climb As described below to the upper Val Grialetsch, then climb the slopes on the right to the pass.

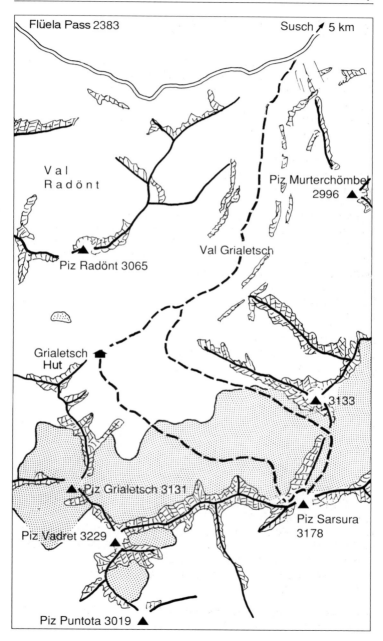

Flüela Pass 2383

Susch 5 km

Val Radönt

Piz Murterchömbel 2996 ▲

Piz Radönt 3065 ▲

Val Grialetsch

Grialetsch Hut ▲

▲ 3133

Piz Grialetsch 3131 ▲

Piz Sarsura 3178 ▲

Piz Vadret 3229 ▲

Piz Puntota 3019 ▲

Direct Ascent via the Fuorcla Sarsura From the lowest point at Chant Sura, go south to a distinct shoulder, where a path begins. Descend this easily into the Val Grialetsch. Walk up the valley past the alp hut on the other side of the stream and at a height of 2260m (no path) climb to the humpback left of the stream. Ascend this for 200m, then make a rather unpleasant traverse to the moraines of the Vadret da Grialetsch. Keeping to the left all the time, cross scree then the gentle glacier slopes to the Fuorcla Sarsura (2923m). Turn a rocky top to the left (east), climb a short, steep step on snow and the splendid open terrain of the Vadret da Sarsura, finishing up a snow ridge to the summit.

Approach from the Hut From the Grialetsch Hut, follow the path south-eastwards across marked moraine country to the Vadret da Grialetsch. Ascend this eastwards, passing either north or south of the Isla Persa, to the small, uppermost glacier basin below and west of the summit. Ascend the steep left hand snow (block) flank to a shoulder on the North Ridge. It is also possible to climb the South-West Ridge (I+).

Descent Variation You can swap routes for the descent.

Piz Vadret seen from the north, across the Vadret da Grialetsch.

Piz Palü, 3905m

Many things play a part in making Piz Palü easily the most famous glacier peak in the Eastern Alps. For one thing there is its unique 900m high North Face with its three pillars and four hanging glaciers, which stand out so ostentatiously for everyone to admire. That famous old film, *White Hell of Piz Palü*, certainly plays its part too. And finally there is the cablecar to the Diavolezza, which brings this objective so close that sometimes whole tapeworms of people are crawling up the very crevassed Pers Glacier in the direction of the summit. Naturally that leads to underestimation of this splendid, yet exacting and very high alpine route.

View of the three summits of Piz Palü and its 900m high North Face. In the foreground is the lower part of the Fortezzagrat.

First Ascents East Peak – O. Heer and party, 1835. C and W. Digby and party 1866. Traverse – Wachtler, Wallner, Georg and party, 1868.
Character and Demands PD/AD (traverse) A popular, high alpine glacier route, with dangerous crevasses, and an exposed knife-edge ridge with enormous cornices in places.
Timings Diavolezza to Piz Palü 4½ hrs.

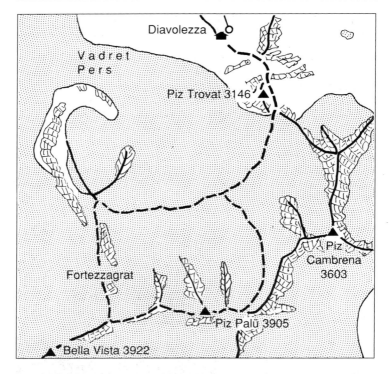

Best Maps Swiss Landeskarte, 1:50,000 Sheet 268, *Julier-pass*; or 1:25,000 Sheet 1257 *Piz Bernina*.

Approach From Pontresina in the Upper Engadine, go up the broad-bottomed Bernina valley to the Diavolezza cablecar station. 081 842 6205
Starting Point The private alpine hut (100 beds ☎ 082 66 205) at Diavolezza (2973m), the top station of the cablecar, offers an impressive view of Piz Palü.
Other Peaks Munt Pers (3207m, 45 mins), an evening stroll from the Diavolezza, provides a magnificent belvedere for the entire panorama of the Morteratsch basin, including Piz Bernina, Biancograt, Piz Palü, etc.
Usual Ascent From the hut, follow tracks south-eastwards to the scree saddle between Sass Queder and Piz Trovat. Traverse the very steep eastern flank of the latter on to the Pers Glacier which is reached at a height of 3000m. Follow the broad track southwards, then work your way up through an impres-

sive icefall into the upper basin with big crevasses and a steep step. Climb just as steeply to the shoulder of the East Ridge and ascend the splendid snow edge to the East Peak (3882m). Then traverse the partly knife-edged and very exposed ridge to the main peak keeping well below any cornices.

Descent This is usually by the same route but you can also traverse Piz Palü to the west (exacting, ice ridges, rock-climbing to III–) and descend the Fortezzagrat (see p33).

The upper Pers Glacier. The eastern shoulder is at the top of the track visible on the left hand side. On the right is the East Peak of Piz Palü with its gigantic cornices.

Piz Morteratsch, 3751m

Piz Morteratsch could be described as a Bernina peak of the second rank as it is a bit lower than the really big ones. It stands on a secondary crest and its ascent is somewhat less demanding. But the peak is quite unjustly left out of many selections because in the entire alps there are few summits that offer views of such quality. From here one can study at leisure the great faces of the highest peaks of the area. One looks straight at the Piz Bernina's fabulous Biancograt, at Piz Scersen with its ice nose, and at the North-East Face of Piz Roseg, with its famous 600m ice face. Directly below is the Tschierva Glacier, so close that, from above, one can almost literally spit into its crevasses. There are equally interesting aspects looking east across the Fortezzagrat to Piz Palü. So the traverse of the peak, up the Morteratsch side and down the Tschierva, not only teaches the climber about the two great glacier basins of the Bernina, but also gives him a chance to admire and study all the famous peaks. And for those hungry for summits, there is still the 'makeweight' Piz Tschierva (3546m).

First Ascent C. Brugger, P. Gensler with K. Emmermann and A. Klaingutti, 1858.
Character and Demands PD– A varied high route with friable rock steps and moderately steep snow slopes, plus some big crevasses.
Timings From Morteratsch to the Boval Hut 2 hrs, to the summit 4 hrs; descent to Tschierva, 2 hrs.
Best Maps Swiss Landeskarte, 1:50,000 Sheet 268 *Julierpass*; or 1:25,000 Sheet 1257 *Piz Bernina*.

Approach From Pontresina in the Upper Engadine, continue 3km southwards towards the Bernina Pass. Now turn off right to Morteratsch (1896m, station, hotel), a very busy starting point for walks and big mountain routes.
Valley Base Pontresina (1805m), one of the best known holiday resorts in the Upper Engadine and starting point for both the principal valleys in the Bernina Group.
Hut Bases Boval Hut (2495m, SAC Bernina Section, 60 beds ☎ 082 66 403); Tschierva Hut (2573m, 100 beds ☎ 082 66 391).
Other Peaks Piz Bernina (4049m) and Bella Vista (3922m).

Hut Climb Leave Morteratsch on the right towards the nearby foot of the mountain and ascend quickly through the woods to

Chunetta, a picturesque top with glacier polished rocks, bizarre pine trees and a marvellous view of Piz Palü. Then continue far up the valley, partly on the big moraine, partly behind it. Finally turn right at a corner and climb up to the huts.

Ascent from Boval From the huts, head due west up over boulders and grass slopes into a high cirque. At a height of 3000m work over to the left and climb quickly up to the edge of the glacier, then up a broken rock step (stonefall!) to the Fuorcla da Boval (3347m), the most used crossing to the Tschierva Hut. Descend over the bergshrund, then continue southwards up the steep slope to the start of the broad snow ridge. Ascend this until you can easily traverse left into the glacier basin. Cross more crevasses, then climb straight up and over a last short ridge on to the south-west jutting summit, below which the rocks fall 900m sheer to the Tschierva Glacier.

Descent to Tschierva Retrace your steps almost to the Fuorcla da Boval. Now descend the broad, flat glacier basin of the Vadrettin da Tschierva. A diversion to climb Piz Tschierva (3546m) takes about 1 hour. On the descent head due west as far as the opposite bank of the glacier. Now descend another 100m, then move to the right to a boulder field at Terrassa (3100m). At its western end a path leads across the rocky slope to the Tschierva Hut. Descend to the Val Roseg and thence to Pontresina where a train can be used to return to Morteratsch.

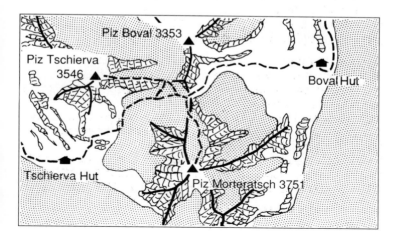

Piz Bernina, 4049m

The only four-thousander in the Eastern Alps fully deserves its position as monarch of all it surveys! In truly Western Alps style, it is covered with a thick and lengthy mantle of ice. High faces fall away on all sides and to the north it sends out the Biancograt, the last word in snowy knife-edges. The long route from the Tschierva Hut up this ridge to the foresummit of Piz Alv (Piz Bianco, 3995m) and on towards the summit of the Bernina is the dream of countless climbers, and is thus very busy. Yet the presence of so many people should not be allowed to lead to carelessness, either on the part of climbers or alpine writers, who nowadays play down its difficulties all too nonchalantly. It is a very long, very serious route at such a height, and one can seldom expect to find bare, dry rock on the final and particularly exposed section of the ridge. Its grading of II-III is perhaps adequate in ideal conditions but it gives a false impression!

If that route is considered too hard the easier ascent from the East and South may be preferred. On this, the Fortezzagrat, with its views of Piz Palü, the enormous crevasses of the Morteratsch Glacier, the fine position of the Marco-e-Rosa Hut and the knife-edged Spallagrat are also sure to impress.

First Ascent F. Tuckett, F. Brown with C. Almer and F. Andermatten, 1866.

Character and Demands PD+ A route across enormous

The Tschierva Glacier with the Biancograt (left), Piz Bernina and Piz Scersen.

glacier slopes with big crevasses and steep steps, and an exposed and sometimes very sharp-edged summit ridge. Settled weather is absolutely necessary on account of the complicated return journey.

Timings To the Boval Hut 2 hrs, from there to the Marco-e-Rosa Hut at least 6 hrs; from the Diavolezza an hour less; summit climb 1½ hrs.

Best Maps Swiss Landeskarte, 1:50,000 Sheet 268 *Julierpass*; or 1:25,000 Sheet 1257 *Piz Bernina*.

Approach From Pontresina in the Upper Engadine, continue for 3km in the direction of the Bernina Pass, then turn off right to Morteratsch (1896m, station, hotel), a very popular starting point for walking and big mountain routes.

Valley Base Pontresina (1805m), one of the best known holiday and mountaineering resorts in the Upper Engadine.

Hut Bases Boval Hut (Chamanna da Boval, 2495m, SAC Bernina Section, 60 beds ☎ 082 66 403) see p30; Marco-e-Rosa Hut (3597m, CAI beds ☎ 0342 21 32 370).
                                                    0039   515

The Marco-e-Rosa Hut climb From the Boval Hut, ascend the valley southwards for 1km, then cross the glacier due east to the left rock foot of the Isla Persa (by the moraine lake). Ascend the path, then continue southwards across the small Vadret da la Fortezza to the start of the Fortezza Ridge. This point also is reached from the Diavolezza (see p28) by traversing the middle Pers Glacier. Ascend the snow ridge (marvellous views!) then a few rock steps (II) to the glacier roof above. Climb straight up for another 200m, then traverse west almost horiontally over the so-called Bella Vista Terrace. Descend very steeply from its western end, then continue westwards below Crast' Agüzza threading between enormous crevasses to gain the Fuorcla Crast' Agüzza, beyond which is the Marco-e-Rosa hut, situated on a rock nose.

The Spallagrat From the hut, start northwards over the firstly flat, then moderately steep snow slope to the beginning of the Spallagrat – the South Ridge of Piz Bernina. Climb a small rock step protected by a steel cable, then follow the crest to La Spalla (4020m). Continue up the very exposed ridge, which sometimes narrows to an arête, to the rocky summit.

Descent Descend by the same route, with a reverse climb up to the Bella Vista Terrace. In especially favourable conditions it is possible, and quicker, to descend (and ascend) the crevassed Labyrinth of the Buuch icefall of the Morteratsch Glacier.

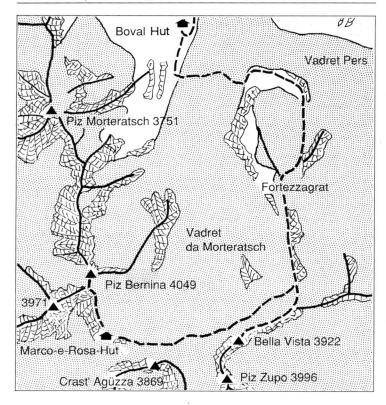

Ascent by the Biancograt The celebrated North Ridge of Piz
Bernina – the Biancograt – is an elegant ice ridge that is tackled
from the Tschierva Hut in the Roseg Valley (approached from
Pontresina). The ridge is straightforward for a well-trained party
but at AD/AD+ is rather harder than the climbs in this guide.
Above the hut the route works up moraines left of the Tschierva
Glacier below the south-western slopes of Piz Morteratsch, then
on to the upper glacier slopes and up to the Fourcla Prievlusa at
the foot of the ridge. The ridge begins with the traverse of a small
outcrop and thereafter the classic snow and ice arête (sometimes corniced) stretches elegantly upwards to the Pont Alv
(3995m). Beyond this the ridge is broken with small gendarmes
and two quite pronounced notches; the first (III+ or abseil) is
followed by a tower (turned on the right or left or crossed directly)
to reach the second gap. Beyond this a steep snow-encrusted
ridge leads to the summit. 8-11 hours from the Tschierva Hut.

Bella Vista, 3922m

The other routes from the Roseg valley in the Bernina Group, either the routes up Piz Roseg (3937m) or Piz Scersen (3971m) are also long and demanding and beyond the scope of this guidebook. So another route on the Morteratsch side has been chosen. The four-topped Bella Vista is actually higher than Piz Palü, and offers a beautiful icy summit ridge with sections of rock-climbing (I+). The Fortezzagrat provides a direct approach so that Bella Vista can be climbed in a day from the Boval or Diavolezza Huts.

First Ascent E. Burckhardt with H. Grass, 1868.
Character and Demands PD A large-scale ice route with some rock (II on the Fortezzagrat) and sharp snow arêtes.
Timings Hut climb 2 hrs, summit climb 5 hrs.
Best Maps / Approach / Valley Base / Hut Base / Hut Climb (see p33).

Summit Climb Proceed as described on p33 over the Isla Persa and the Fortezzagrat. From the end of the latter, climb straight up the glacier to the snow saddle between the first two Bella Vista summits. Turn right and ascend the second peak (3893m), an elegant slice of ice and move on along the snow arête to the third peak, then climb a short, straightforward rock arête to the highest point.

Cima di Rosso, 3366m

This route up Cima di Rosso over the Forno basin should be stimulating. In the most important rock region in the Eastern Alps, there is also a string of really impressive glacier objectives: the Cima dal Cantun (3354m), the Pizzo di Zocca (3174m) and the Cima della Bondasca (3289m) are all superb and many will regret the omission of the second highest peak in the range, Cima di Castello (3392m). This magnificent, four-cornered rock peak offers a much more exacting alternative to the Rosso route, via its North Ridge (PD+ II/III) which can also be climbed from the Forno Hut.

Now to the Cima di Rosso itself, with its high northern ice face plunging in two sections, a really scary picture during the approach. For that reason, it is necessary to make a long glacier detour to get at it from behind. This is doubly impressive, firstly for the uncommonly steep Torrone (3349m), adorned with ice, and the wildly broken glacier, where one must search for a way up. Those who are fit enough can finish by paying a visit to Monte Sissone (3330m), which is reached in about 45 minutes via the col separating it from Cima di Rosso.

First Ascent W. Coolidge with F. and H. Devoussoud, 1867.
Character and Demands PD− This is one of the most impressive glacier routes in this book, both steep and much crevassed.
Timings From Maloja to the hut 3½ hrs, from there to Cima di Rosso likewise about 3½ hrs, depending very much on the conditions.
Best Maps Swiss Landeskarte, 1:50,000 Sheets 268 *Julierpass* and 278 *Monte Disgrazia.*

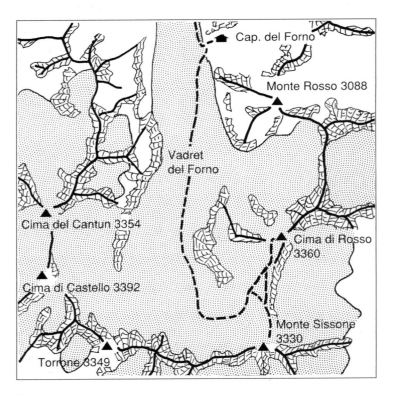

Approach To St. Moritz in the Upper Engadine and on past the lakes to Maloja and the Maloja Pass (1815m).

Valley Base Maloja, the last habitation in the Upper Engadine, just south of the Silsersee before the sudden drop down to the Bregaglia. Beautiful views of the mountains.

Hut Base Forno Hut (2574m, SAC Rorscach Section ☎ 082 43 182).

Other Peaks Monte del Forno (3214m), a quite separate rock peak, with beautiful climbing up its South Ridge (II), 2 hrs.

Hut Climb Where the Maloja Pass road begins to descend in the direction of Bregaglia, turn off on to the hut path. Climb up across meadows and through woods to the much visited and photographed Calvoc Lake. Continue on the flat southwards, then turn into the narrow Fornotal and ascend moraine scree to the snout of the glacier. Climb steeply at first, then moderately, going up the glacier, finally turning left to cross moraines and some rock to reach the Forno Hut, which stands some 100m above the glacier in the most beautiful situation.

Summit Climb Go back down to the Forno Glacier and continue southwards up the level glacier for almost 3km towards the rugged Torrone summits. Then turn left where the glacier rears up steeply at a height of 2800m. Now it is best to ascend the middle of the glacier to about 3000m, then turn left into the upper basin and, without further problem, ascend to the uppermost part of the West Ridge and the summit.

Monte Disgrazia, 3678m

Monte Disgrazia is like no other mountain, a peak with a perfect shape, of elemental power, savage, inaccessible and adorned with broken glaciers. The principal peak in the Bregaglia rises completely isolated, only connected with the main chain by a deeply notched ridge. The striking Italian name means 'Peak of Misfortune'.

From most aspects it appears quite difficult, with its long ridges and high, ferocious faces. But there is just one relatively easy approach hidden away to the south-west where the Preda Rossa Glacier allows one to reach high on the North-West Ridge. This is a very long knife-edge (mixed, with icy sections) which falls away down fierce faces, particularly northwards. Therefore, not only is high alpine experience required, but the difficulties are heavily dependent on the prevailing conditions. All the other routes are substantially harder. Among these is the Spigalo Inglese up the 500m North Face, which was first climbed in 1910 by Ling and Raeburn. It is a pure ice route (D) with sections up to 55°, which goes up the rib to the right of the North Face Direct route, a rather more demanding excursion (TD) first climbed by Albertini and Schenatti in 1934. Rather easier than these savage routes is the Corda Molla (North-North-East Ridge) a remote and elegant mixed climb (AD+) approached from the Porro Hut and the Taveggia bivouac hut above Chiareggia in Val Malenco. Good though the north side routes are, they are all too hard for this guide which leaves the Preda Rossa route the only feasible recommendation.

First Ascent L. Stephen, E. Kennedy, T. Cox with A. Anderegg, 1862.
Character and Demands PD+ Relatively easy as far as the saddle (Sella di Pioda) despite the steep snow. Then a long, sharp-edged, and in part exposed, ridge (to II+), which – according to conditions – is spiced with snow or ice sections.
Timings From Preda Rossa to the hut 2 hrs, from there to the summit 4 hrs.
Best Map Swiss Landeskarte, 1:50,000 Sheet 278 *Monte Disgrazia*.

Approach From Valtalinna, which runs east from the head of Lake Como head north from Masino to Cataeggio and thence by the Val di Sasso Bisolo to large car parking areas at the Preda Rossa meadows (1960m).
Valley Base Cataeggio (791m) a village halfway up the Val Masino.
Hut Base Rifugio Cesare Ponti (2559m, CAI, 40 beds ☎ 0342 611455).

Hut Climb Walk through pasture slopes from Preda Rossa, then up a steep step on the left, above which long rising traverse leads to the hut (2 hrs).

Ordinary Route Climb the rocky slopes or the moraine left of the Preda Rossa Glacier to the upper end of the moraine. Get onto the glacier and climb to the bergschrund, keeping all the time on the left hand side of the glacier, and then go steeply up

to the saddle of Sella di Pioda (3387m). Climb the long and
exposed North-West Ridge (with detours on the right to avoid
big cornices on the left) to a foresummit after which a narrow
ridge of mixed ground leads to the highest point. (4-5 hrs from
the Ponti Hut.)

Descent Descend by the same route.

Variation PD From below the final slopes to the Sella move
left and gain the lowest rocks of the South-West Ridge which
can be followed to the top (mixed, some stonefall danger).

*Monte Disgrazia from Monte Sissone with the Corda Molla on the left, the North Face in the centre,
and the upper part of the Predo Rossa route following the ridge to the summit from the prominent
Sella di Pioda on the right. The Predo Rossa approach is hidden beyond the right hand ridge.*

Ortler and Adamello Groups

The Ortler Group is a knot of fine high mountains situated in a corner of northern Italy near the borders of Austria and Switzerland most readily accessible from the north from Landeck in the Inn Valley, or by travelling west from the Italian side of the Brenner Pass. As part of South Tirol this is a German/Italian speaking area and the German names predominate.

The Ortler (Cima Ortles), Königspitze (Gran Zebru) and Monte Cevedale are the dominant peaks in the centre of the range but there are a number of excellent satellite peaks including those around Sulden and Trafoi in the North but also those approached by the valleys that radiate from the southern part of the range.

Everywhere there are mighty peaks with spacious glacier approaches that add stature to their beautiful and distinctive appearance. The dramatic peaks around the Ortler (crumbly limestone), with its very rugged build, high faces and enormous scree slopes, are fundamentally different from the peaks in the southern part of the range (gneiss, schists) which have rather more sedate profiles.

Apart from the six peaks described in this region another dozen are worthy of inclusion, including easy objectives like the Höhe Schneide (3434m) by the Stelvio Pass, which can be suitably combined with its neighbours; ridge routes like the traverse of Cima Venezia (3386m); such a splendid glacier trip as the passage of the Unterer Ortler Glacier and the North-West Ridge to the Grosser Eiskogel (3530m) and other high peaks such as Monte Zebru (3735m) situated between the Ortler and the Königspitze.

I have also included in this section the high mountain groups of Presanella and Adamello south of the Sondrio/Bolzano road in the locality of the Tonale Pass. The tonalite rocks hereabouts create beautiful and, in places, very rugged mountain formations in a genuine glacier massif, dominated by the Cima Presanella. Things are different, however, in the Adamello region, the last big central alpine massif to the south. Above the broad, mostly flat snow basins, soar many easily climbable peaks, of which Monte Adamello (3554m) is the highest and most striking. Thanks to the highly placed Lobbia Hut (3020m), its ascent can be included as part of an extensive itinerary.

In the following pages the heights on the official Italian maps are used in preference to the totally outdated German-Austrian measurements.

On the way from the Schaubach Hut to the Casati Hut, with a view
of the Sulden Glacier and the Kreilspitze. ▷

Vertainspitze, 3545m
(Cima Vertana)

The slight glaciation of the really stately peaks above the Zaytal catches the eye. These mountains lie in the rain shadow of their big neighbours to the south-west with glaciers on their north-east flanks. The Vertainspitze ranks as the principal peak amongst the glacier routes and whilst you are tackling that you can easily take in the second big peak in the group, the Hoher Angelus (3521m) as the high position of the Düsseldorf Hut (Rifugio Serristori) makes this possible. This friendly hut is situated in a singular spot. Its magic comes from its immediate surroundings of an enormous boulder landscape, interspersed with small grassy flats and pools and in the background the North Faces of the Ortler and Königspitze dominate the scene. Moreover, the hut warden is very active, having fully equipped the North-West Ridge of the Vertainspitze (PD) (and other peaks in the area) with all the paraphernalia of protection.

First Ascent (South-East Ridge) J. Payer with J. Pinggera, 1865.
Character and Demands PD/F Some steep places on the Zay Glacier, and rock ridges no harder than I.
Timings From the Kanzel (Il Pulpito) to the hut 1½ hrs; via the Angelusscharte (Passo dell'Angelo) to the summit about 2½ hrs; and from the col to the top of the Hoher Angelus 40 mins.
Best Maps 1:25,000 Tabacco, *Ortler Group*; or Touring Club Italiano, 1:50,000 Sheet D62 *Gruppo Ortles Cevedale*.

Approach In Spondigna (Spondinig) in the upper Val Venosta, take the Stelvio Pass road through Prad to Gomagoi, then turn left for Sulden (Solda), 22km.
Valley Base Sulden (1857m), a famous climbers' haunt with splendid mountain scenery and a big choice of high routes.
Hut Base The beautifully situated Düsseldorf Hut (Zaytal Hut or Rifugio Serristori, 2721m, CAI, ☎ 0473 ~~75515~~). 613115
Other Peaks Tschenglser Hochwand (Croda di Cengles, 3375m, 2 hrs), an interesting and relatively harmless rock-climb.
Hut Climb From the highest part of Sulden, take the chairlift to the Kanzel (2350m). Follow a broad path across the slopes, then cross a Cyclops-like boulder-field, finishing up a steep step to the hut, which is visible from far off.

Vertainspitze via the Angelusscharte Behind the hut, take the right hand fork in the path to a lake and traverse moraine slopes to the southern Zay Glacier. Ascend this somewhat to the left. Climb energetically past the northern side of the rock island which divides the glacier in two, and steeply up to the Angelusscharte (3337m). Turn the first drop on the North-East Ridge on the left, then ascend the rather long drawn-out and jagged, snow and boulder ridge (some belays) to the summit. (Should this ridge be icy, then one can cross the col on to the Laaser Glacier and traverse to the Rosimjoch, to ascend the South-East Ridge. F)

Hoher Angelus (3521m) This beautiful rock and ice peak is most easily climbed from the Angelusscharte. Just follow the moderate block and snow ridge. Those who prefer a traverse of both mountains starting with the Hoher Angelus will use the 'Reinstadlerroute'. This starts at the snout of the southern Zay Glacier where one should turn north on to the moraine and ascend to the foot of the North-West Ridge. The ridge is way-marked and steel cable protects a steep step beyond which pleasant snow or block climbing leads to the summit.

Vertainspitze Descent If returning to Sulden, the best descent is by the easy South-East Ridge to the Rosimjoch (Passo di Rosim). From there, skirt the right hand side of the Rosim Glacier to get down into the Rosim valley which can either be followed all the way down or quit (right) to use the chairlift.

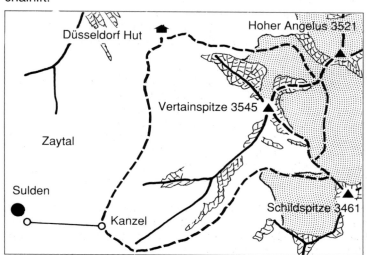

Königspitze, 3851m
(Gran Zebru)

The Ortler owes its imposing appearance to its height, bulk and free-standing position. The Königspitze, though only 50m lower, relies more on elegance! Its celebrated North Face, composed of rock and smoothly chiselled ice, above is enhanced by the wild cascades of the Königswand Glacier. It is the showpiece of the Sulden valley! But the peak is also beautiful from the south-east, cone-shaped with very steep flanks and here the South-East Ridge provides the most reasonable ascent. It is best to climb the peak early in the season as ice covers the middle section of ridge and it is not difficult to imagine the feeling of exposure at this point. If there is a good track on firm snow this passage is straightforward, whereas in the bare ice, sometimes found in late season, the ridge can become particularly dangerous.

The proper base for the Königspitze is the popular Pizzini Hut which is easily reached from the Val di Cedec, the uppermost section of the Valfurva to the south. One can also start from Sulden by way of the Casati Hut or the Cedlo Pass, but this is illogical involving a three hour climb up the very crevassed Sulden Glacier and a 300m descent from the Casati Hut into the Val di Cedec before the climb proper begins. Good climbers can shorten this by using the Cedec Pass (3238m), but everyone should avoid the stonefall menaced Königsjoch (Passo Bottiglia) used on the first ascent this side of the mountain.

People have been quarrelling about the first ascent of this striking peak for over a hundred years. The cleric Stefan Steinberger speaking of his grand tour in 1854, recorded that he had climbed the Königspitze from the Stelvio Pass by the South-West Gully – a fantastic performance, if the story is true!

First Ascent F. Tuckett, E. Buxton with C. Michel and F. Biner, 1864.

Character and Demands PD A big and very high alpine mountain route with little glacier work but a steep snow slope (up to 40°) in an exposed position, moderate rock, but very dependent on conditions, and very popular.

The view of the Königspitze from the east-north-east with its famous North Face in shadow, and the riven Königswand Glacier below on the right. The sunlit South-East Ridge is in profile on the left. ▷

Timings Approach to the Pizzini Hut 1¾ hrs; to the summit 4-5 hrs; from the Casati Hut, about 4 hrs.
Best Maps Tabacco, 1:25,000 Sheet *Ortler Group*; or *Touring Club Italiano*, 1:50,000 Sheet D62 *Gruppo Ortles Cevedale*.

Approach To Bormio from the Val Venosta in the north via the Stelvio Pass; or quicker (if coming from Switzerland), along the Münstertal and over the Umbrail Pass. From Bormio, it is another 13km to Santa Caterina Valfurva (1734m), the best starting point for the big Ortler climbs (an even better choice than Sulden!).
Starting point From Santa Caterina, ascend the Val Forno for 6km to the Albergo Forno (2170m), starting point for the Pizzini, Casati and Branca Huts.
Hut Base Rifugio Pizzini (2700m, CAI, 80 beds ☎ 0342 935513) on the broad valley bottom of the upper Val di Cedec, with impressive views of Monte Cevedale and Monte Pasquale with their steep glaciers.

Hut Climb From the Albergo Forno, continue up the Val di Cedec to the Rifugio Pizzini on a broad and much used path.

Summit Climb From the hut, walk northwards across the broad valley bottom to the Gran Zebru Glacier. Ascend this heading north-east to gain the Königsjoch (Passo Bottiglia). (This point can be reached from the Casati Hut after a descent and a traverse below the Suldenspitze and Kreilspitze.) Climb straight up a rock (snow) rib on to the lower shoulder. Now ascend the very steep, 400m high(!) slopes of the broad snow/ice ridge, past the upper shoulder, to the summit ridge, which gradually relents.

Descent Descend with care by the same route.

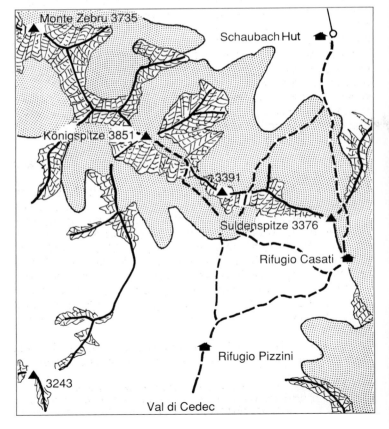

Ortler, 3905m
(Cima Ortles)

Together with the Gross Glockner, the Ortler is certainly the most famous peak in the Eastern Alps. Its position contributes fundamentally to its popularity. The Ortler greets drivers coming from the north just beyond the Reschenpass. It looms over the waters of the Reschensee like a round, white dome, a prototype of the 'eternal mountains'. Yet in reality the ravages of time gnaw at it more fiercely than many other massifs – its loose rocks assisting a remorseless alpine weathering.

Its grey dolomite-limestone is a rather brittle rock that crumbles to splintery scree. This becomes very apparent on the approach from the top of the chairlift at Langenstein to one of the two huts where the snouts of the Marlt and Ende-der-Welt Glaciers are so thickly overlaid with scree that they cannot be distinguished from the moraines. Nevertheless, the ice ensures that the ascent of the Ortler is one of the most splendid in this book. On the ordinary route from the Payer Hut, it is the enormous, very varied and promising upper Ortler Glacier which makes it so special. On the Hintergrat, a completely glacier free ascent, it is the sharp-edged snow ridges which impress. The combination of both routes provides a climb of western alpine stature.

First Ascent E. & H. Buxton, F. Tuckett with C. Michel and F. Biner, 1868.

Character and Demands PD The Ortler Glacier Route is an impressive high alpine route over a big glacier with crevasses and steep steps, yet not too technically demanding; very exposed to the weather (storm) conditions, and very popular. The East-South-East Ridge or Hintergrat (Coston di Dentro) PD+ is substantially harder, with rock-climbing on splintery rock to II+, long snow ridges, and in some parts very exposed.

Timings From Langenstein to the Payer Hut 3 hrs, glacier ascent of the Ortler 3-4 hrs; from Langenstein to the Hintergrat (or Coston) Hut 1½ hrs, ascent of the Ortler via the Hintergrat, about 5 hrs.

Best Maps Tabacco, 1:25,000 Sheet *Ortler Group*; or *Touring Club Italiano*, 1:50,000 Sheet D62 *Gruppo Ortles Cevedale*.

Overleaf: A view of the Ortler massif from the vicinity of the Payer Hut. Below the highest point is the North Face, with top right the Ortler Glacier, on the front part of which (centre right) can be seen the tracks of the ordinary route. ▷

Approach / Valley Base See p42.

Hut Bases Payer Hut (3029m, CAI, 70 beds ☎ 0473 75410) in an unusual position on the Tabaretta crest with clear views in three directions; Hintergrat Hut (2661m, private, 60 beds), situated by a mountain lake, close to the very impressive North Faces of Monte Zebru and the Königspitze.

Ascent to the Payer Hut At the beginning of Sulden, before the bridge over the river, turn right from the main road down to the Langenstein chairlift and ride this up to the top (2330m).

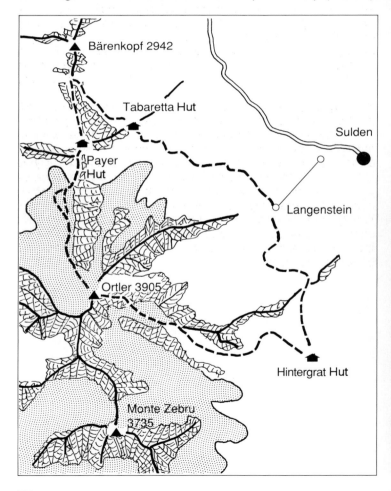

Descend slightly northwards into the rubble-filled Marlttal below the Ortler North Face and ascend the opposite side of the valley to the Tabaretta Hut (2556m, private, 50 beds), which is sited on a rib in the terrain. Continue beyond the hut up scree slopes to a shattered rock slope and over broken rocks to the Bären Pass (2871m). Now follow the ridge southwards, either on it or near the crest, to the Payer Hut. There is a distinct path all the way.

Ortler Glacier Route (Tabaretta Route) Ascend a little path over scree and crumbly rock (and eventually snowfields), turning the Tabarettaspitze to gain the notch beyond it and on to the rocks of the Tschirfeck. Follow the belays up the rock wall to the upper Ortler Glacier. Now either climb straight up or swing right through the Barenloch basin to the ruined Lombardi Bivouac. Climb a steep step in the glacier, then traverse the broad slopes to the summit, which rises only slightly above the surrounding ice.

Hintergrat (Coston di Dentro) From the Langenstein chairlift (2330m), traverse the rubble-filled Ende-der-Welt cirque at the foot of the Ortler East Face and contour around the spurs of the Hintergrat to the Hintergrat Hut. Ascend a path, then on climbers' tracks up steep scree and snow slopes for a long way to the Oberer Knott (3466m). Follow a long snow ridge towards the Signalkopf, then on the left of the brittle rock slope, climb over ledges and up gullies (steel cables) to the ridge beyond. Finally traverse some small ridge tops over mixed ground (very exposed in places) to the summit.

Descent Descend via the glacier route to the Payer Hut and back to Langenstein.

Monte Cevedale, 3769m

Together with the almost as high Zufallspitze, Monte Cevedale makes up the beautiful tent-shaped glacier ridge which soars far above the other peaks of the southern Ortler Group. The ascent from the Casati Hut over the kilometre-wide glacier ridge can be classified as moderate, especially since there is always a deep track leading up it. Only at the summit is there a bergschrund and a short steep slope. The high starting hut suggests an extension of the route: the Zufallspitze is quickly reached; one can easily traverse to Monte Pasquale (3553m) and descend its South-West Ridge; or finally one could follow the 'Haute Route' along an arresting ridge (no serious difficulty) to Monte Vioz (3645m) and thereby bag three big Ortler peaks in one day!

First Ascent J. Payer with J. Pinggera, 1865; traverse to Monte Vioz (first done in the opposite direction) F. Tuckett, D. Freshfield and party, 1865.

Character and Demands F+ A beautiful and, in relation to its height, moderate glacier route up an outstanding peak, with a bergschrund and short steep slope below the ridge. For the traverse to Monte Vioz (PD), settled weather conditions are imperative, otherwise it can be dangerous!

Timings Hut climb, 3 hrs; Casati Hut to Monte Cevedale 1½ to 2 hrs; traverse to Monte Vioz at least 4 hrs.

Best Map Touring Club Italiano, 1:50,000 Sheet D62 *Gruppo Ortles Cevedale* .

Approach / Starting Point See p45.

Hut Base Rifugio Casati (3270m, CAI, 230 beds ☎ 0342 935507), a very handsome building at the edge of the glacier near the Passo di Cevedale, a decidely popular goal for walkers.

Other Peaks Suldenspitze (3376m), a sedate mountain reached from the hut (30 minutes) via an easy mixed ridge.

Hut Climb From the Albergo Forno, ascend the Cedec valley north-westwards above the stream to the Rifugio Pizzini (2700m, see p45). Then across scree bottoms to the foot of the high step and steeply up the well-trodden path to the hut. An ascent from the Schaubach Hut, at the top of the cablecar from

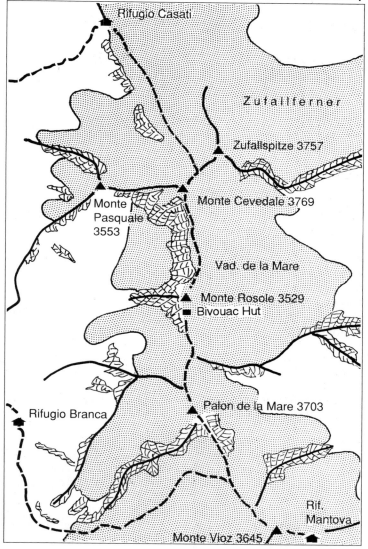

Sulden, over the Sulden Glacier (many crevasses!) and the Eissee Pass takes 3 hours.

Summit Climb The route follows the broad glacier roof all the way up the Cevedale massif. At the foot of the steep slopes, keep more to the right, cross two crevasses and ascend a slope on to the ridge. Continue south-westwards, rather exposed at the end, to the top of Monte Cevedale. If the sharp snow ridge is followed north-eastwards, it takes 15 minutes to reach the Zufallspitze.

Traverse to Monte Vioz Descend the obvious South Ridge of Monte Cevedale for a long way to the first saddle and over a small top into the Passo Rosole (3502m). Climb Monte Rosole (3529m) and then descend its rocky South Ridge to the Rosole bivouac hut by the Col de la Mare (3442m). Ascend the broad glacier crest on to Pallon de la Mare (3703m). Then make a steep, block-like descent into the Passo della Vedretta Rossa (3405m), the lowest point on the ridge. The final climb, again over a spacious glacier crest, is up on to Monte Vioz (3645m). To the south-east, is the slightly lower Rifugio Mantova di Vioz (3535m, CAI, 50 beds ☎ 0463 71386). This traverse from Monte Cevedale has no technical difficulties but is still a route at very great height! and therefore potentially serious. If returning to Valfurva one can descend Monte Vioz down the very crevassed Forno Glacier to the Rifugio Branca, or easier, begin the descent from the Pallon de la Mare. Good climbers also continue the traverse from Monte Vioz over four more high peaks to Punta San Matteo (see p56), but this extension is more demanding than the traverse from Monte Cevedale.

Monte Cevedale, on the left is the roof-like glacier of the ordinary route.

Cima Venezia, 3386m

Here are just a few lines to stimulate enthusiasm for this route, perhaps the most interesting in the south-east of the region. The approach is by the fascinating, somewhat austere Val Martello, a very popular valley that penetrates to the east of the range.

First Ascent J. Payer with J. Pinggera.
Character and Demands PD– A glacier route, then a snow and block ridge (one section II–), and eventually a large-scale traverse.
Timings To the hut 1½ hrs, from there to Cima Venezia 3 hrs.
Best Map Touring Club Italiano, 1:50,000 Sheet D62 *Gruppo Ortles Cevedale*.

Approach From Coldrano (Goldrain) in the Val Venosta drive up the Val Martello to the car park at the road end.
Hut Base Marteller Hut (2610m, AVS, 60 beds).

Hut Climb From the 'Paradiso' car park go up to the Corsi (Zufall) Hut (2265m, CAI, ☎ 0473 71110), then turn south, cross the stream and ascend a slope to the new hut.
Summit Climb Climb the slopes eastwards and get on to the Hohen Glacier at a height of about 3000m. Ascend the glacier easily to the Cima Marmotta (3330m). Proceed north-east towards Cima Venezia, either on the ridge, or more easily to a notch on the right, and a rocky arête to the summit.
Descent Descend the same way or traverse the three peaks of Cima Venezia to the Schranjoch and make a direct descent of the Schran Glacier to the Corsi Hut.

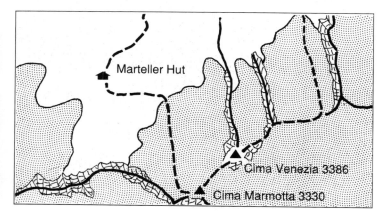

Marteller Hut

Cima Venezia 3386

Cima Marmotta 3330

Punta San Matteo, 3675m

The Forno Glacier (Ghiacciaio dei Forno) is well known to mountaineers and much respected by them. It fills a 6km broad basin and impresses one with its enormous crevasses and big icefalls. Eleven ice peaks, all over 3500m in height, surround it in a semi-circle. Each of them would be a suitable objective for this guidebook. They could all be climbed without any problems were it not for the aforementioned crevasses. The most elegant in form is Punta San Matteo with its 500m North Face of ice. This peak is most conveniently reached by three routes and of these the least known is also the least complicated. You could ascend the Forno Glacier from the Rifugio Bianca or, from there, or from the Rifugio Mantova take the long south westerly ridge over four big peaks (see also under Monte Covedale). But the route offered here is a westerly approach from the Gavia Pass road utilising the Dosegu Glacier, a subtle back-door way free from a lot of the problems of the Forno routes.

First Ascent F. Tuckett, D. Freshfield, J. Backhouse, H. Fox with F. Devouassoud and P. Michel, 1865.

Character and Demands PD– An interesting high route, with a broken glacier and a steeper, exposed snow ridge.

Timings From the road to the summit, a good 4 hrs.

Best Map Touring Club Italiano, 1:50,000 Sheet D62 *Gruppo Ortles Cevedale*.

Approach See p45.

Punta San Matteo with its North Face and the Forno Glacier.

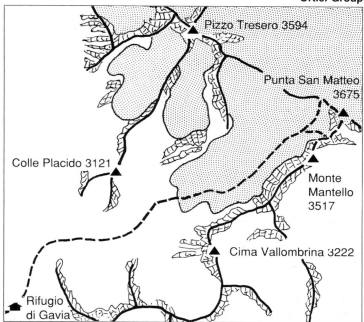

Starting Point Follow the twisting Gavia Pass road as far as the Rifugio Berni (2541m, CAI) situated in the last bottom before the rise to the pass, an 11km drive.

Summit Climb Cross the Gavia stream to the nearby, closed Gavia Hut. Proceed a short distance to the north, then turn off right up the Dosegu valley. Climb two steps to the snout of the Dosegu Glacier. Ascend the southern edge of the glacier and pass the big icefall on the right to gain the upper basin. Continue on the flat to the North-West Ridge. Traverse an intermediate top, then climb steeply up the ridge (cornices) to the summit.

Descent It is possible to descend the rocky South-West Ridge to the lowest notch, and from there make a short detour to Monte Mantello (3517m), before rejoining the route of ascent on the Dosegu Glacier. [*Editor's Note:* A more ambitious alternative is to extend the climb up the Dosego Ridge (PD) to Pizzo Tresero (3602m) and then descend its corniced North-West Ridge (PD) (or the easier South-West Ridge) to the abandoned Bernasconi Hut and thence back to the Gavia Pass road. The British guide to this area advocates this route in the opposite direction – the whole expedition being highly rated, but with an additional 2½ hours required for the approach from the Berni Hut it may no longer be convenient.]

Monte Adamello, 3554m

Enormous, almost flat ice slopes on the north-eastern side and steep drops in all other directions. Such is the character of the Adamello range, the last big glacier massif to the south in the Eastern Alps. Monte Adamello rises a good 100m above its neighbours and really dominates its surroundings. Italians love this soaring peak (as seen from the south) and the congestion in August in the huts is correspondingly great. The guide describes the route from Val Genova to the north-east, a grand valley with rushing streams, waterfalls, and striking angular faces and boulders.

First Ascent J. Payer, Catturani, 1864.

Character and Demands F A very broad glacier approach (crevasses), on which good cold conditions and settled weather are imperative. The final ascent is a long mixed ridge, easy in good conditions, but with some cornices near the top.

Timings Approach to the Lobbia Hut 4 hrs and the summit climb 4 hrs.

Best Map Touring Club Italiano, 1:50,000 Sheet D63 *Gruppo Adamello-Presanella*.

Approach From Carisolo 10km south of Madonna di Campiglio, on the Merano/Brescia road, go west up the Val Genova.

Starting Point By car to the waterfalls at Nardis, then by taxi right up the rest of Val Genova to the Rifugio Bedole (1641m).

Hut Base Rifugio Lobbia (3020m, CAI, 120 beds ☎ 0465 52615), situated in an impressive spot amidst the vast high altitude ice sheets.

Hut Climb Cross the Sarca di Genova stream by the Rifugio Bedole and head south for a short way. Then ascend a track and small path up the high rocky step into the upper cirque and traverse moraine scree to the Lobbia Glacier. Start off heading south-west and finally (beyond P.3015) head west to the Lobbia Alta Pass, above which stands the hut.

Summit Climb Firstly, descend easily from the Lobbia saddle, then climb gently south-westwards up the gigantic Mandrone Glacier, passing left of Corno Bianco, then go up to the prominent East Ridge of Monte Adamello and follow this, with the fierce North Face on the right, over snow and blocks to the summit. It is also possible to traverse below the summit slope in order to climb the South Ridge (easier but further).

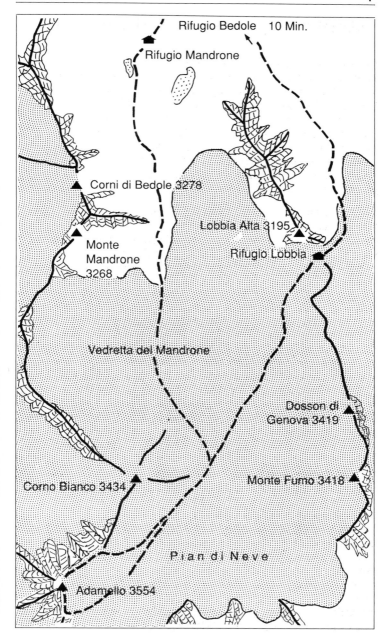

Descent to the Mandrone Hut From the summit, return to the foot of the Corno Bianco by the same route. Now descend due north-east, passing left of an icefall, down to the north-western bank of the glacier. Follow the path across moraines and then grassy slopes to the Mandrone Hut (2449m, CAI ☎ 0465 51193) in a decidely beautiful spot by the Mandrone lakes. Take the customary hut path back to the Rifugio Bedole in the Val Genova.

Alternative Itinerary A useful tactical plan is to climb the mountain from the Mandrone Hut and on the return spend a night at the high Lobbia Hut. In this way one has the choice on the following day of either climbing some more big peaks or doing the glacier route southwards to Care Alto (3462m).

Cima Presanella, 3558m

This is an important peak situated between the Ortler Group to the north and the Adamello massif to the south. While travelling up the Val di Sole to the Tonale Pass, one is greeted with an inspiring sight. Above the short Presanella valley gleams the Cima Presanella with its 500m North Face of ice, which passes on to the even mightier rock walls of the Cima di Vermiglio (3458m). At their feet lies the Denza Hut, one of three Presanella bases. However, the preferred route is not by this arresting frontal approach but from the posh new Segantini Hut to the east. Here too the scenery is impressive: beautiful glacier polished rocks and mountain lakes in the vicinity of the hut and uncommonly rugged, almost black rock peaks, such as Monte Nero (3344m) and Ago di Nardis (3289m). Another advantage of this easterly route is that with the same general approach it could be easily combined with the Adamello itinerary.

First Ascent Unknown, 1859.
Character and Demands A varied high route with short glacier sections, easy climbing on a block-like rock and a snow ridge.
Timings Hut climb 1 hr, summit climb 4 hrs.
Best Map Touring Club Italiano, 1:50,000 Sheet D63 *Gruppo Adamello-Presanella*.

Approach From St. Antonio, 7km south of Madonna di Campiglio on the Merano/Brescia road.

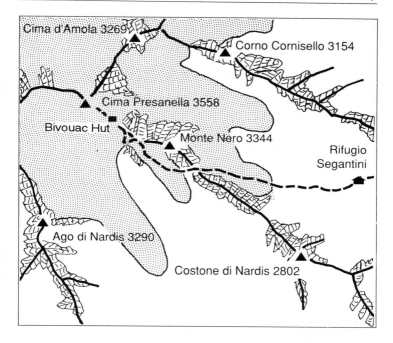

Starting Point From San Antonio, ascend the Valle di Nambrone, then up impressive rock slopes with a left turn at the highest bend to the road end at Vallina d'Amola (2021m).
Hut Base Rifugio Segantini (2373m, CAI, 50 beds ☎ 0465 40384), which also has a good view across the main valley to the Brenta Dolomites.

Hut Climb From the road end, climb the broad path up a slope and crest in the terrain to the hut.
Summit Climb Cross broad bottomed valleys, then cross the moraine to the small southern section of the Amola Glacier. Ascend westwards to the Bocchetta di Monte Nero (3162m), a very impressive saddle, flanked by enormous smooth square blocks of tonalite (a kind of granite). Descend a step on the other side to a separate (eastern) arm of the Nardis Glacier. Climb obliquely to the ridge bordering the left hand side and ascend it to the main crest. Contour left around a rock step to the Orobica Bivouac Hut and climb the ridge, the upper part of which is snow-covered, to the summit.
Descent Descend by the same route.

Ötztal and Stubai Alps

These are two of the most popular mountain areas of the Austrian Tirol; conveniently situated just south of the Inn Valley. In many ways they resemble one another. Mighty mountain crests, each with spines of big, precipitous and inaccessible rock peaks up to 3500m, running northwards. Similarly, somewhat shorter and gentler ridges run southwards, in the Stubai more south-eastwards, which despite their height (up to 3400m) are only modestly glaciated. Nevertheless, in the central sections of both ranges one finds the greatest expanses of ice in all Tirol. There are some fifteen extensive glacier basins, surrounded by dozens of peaks most of which offer an abundance of routes without serious difficulties though the crevasses in the glaciers are an ever present danger, though never bad enough to prevent these ranges being extremely popular for alpine ski tours. What follows is naturally only a selection of climbs from such a rich source. Each hut leads to a multiplicity of objectives and traverses from one base to the next seldom involving problems. This is particularly suitable for the 'stop and go' system: one, two or three peaks from one hut, on to the next hut, routes from there, etc., etc. Indeed the big peaks can be climbed in the course of such traverses, thus making up a kind of 'Haute Route', of several of the biggest peaks like Similaun, Weisskugel and Wildspitze.

In addition to the routes described there are also some more lesser-known objectives that are worth consideration and might be combined with the described routes. In the Ötztal Alps: Langtaufererspitze (3528m) from the Weisskugel Hut; Hinterer Brochkogel (3628m) from the Vernagt or Breslauer Huts; Weisser Kogel (3409m) from the Braunschweiger Hut; Rötenspitze (3393m) from the Martin-Busch Hut and Liebner-spitze (3399m) from the Schönwies Hut. In the Stubai Alps: Sonklarspitze (3467m) from the Becherhaus, Siegerland Hut; Schrandele (3392m) from the Amberger Hut and Seespitzen (3416m) from the Franz-Senn or Regensburger Huts.

The steep icefalls of the Sulzenau Glacier with the Zuckerhütl beyond with its East Ridge on the left and, the ridge leading to the Pfaffenschneide (3498m) on the right. ▷

Wildspitze, 3768m

The highest peak in the Tirol, rising far above its surroundings, looks rather grey and insignificant from the south and east. All the more impressive then is the northern side, where a flawless ice face soars above the icefalls of the Taschach Glacier. There are no less than four huts and five ordinary routes to choose from for the ascent of this popular mountain. All these converge at the foot of the upper section of the South-West Ridge, a veritable alpine crossroads where the great confusion of comings and goings should surprise no one.

In the absence of bare ice (below the steep Mitterkarjoch and on the summit ridge) the mountain can be climbed in a problem-free, three-hour, ascent from the Breslauer Hut. This is the easiest route and the most tedious and is easily followed without a detailed description. For that reason, in this book the absolute opposite is described: the approach by traverse of the Petersenspitze, which takes in glaciers, high snowfields and ice ridges, an itinerary reminiscent of the Midi/Plan traverse and similar excursions in the Western Alps, and which is correspondingly long and exacting. This way also takes in the Taschachtal which is the most impressive valley of the Ötztal Alps. [*Editor's Note:* The climb can be further embellished by adding an ascent of the impressive, but not large, Hinterer Brochkogel, ascending either by the West Ridge (II) or the slightly harder North Ridge and descending the South-East Ridge.]

First Ascent L. Klotz and companion, 1848/61. First traverse inc. Petersenspitze, H. Hess and L. Purtscheller, 1887.
Character and Demands PD One of the big, classic high routes in the Eastern Alps, yet in good conditions without difficult sections, apart from an interesting knife-edge snow ridge on the Petersenspitze. Fine weather essential!
Timings To the Taschachhaus 2½ hrs, to the summit 5 hrs.
Best Map AV-Karte, 1:25,500 Sheet 30/6 *Ötztal Alps Wildspitze*.

Approach From Imst in the Inn Valley go up the Pitztal to the road end at Mittelberg (1736m, 37km).
Starting Point Mittelberg, a once quiet hamlet now transformed by the building of the Pitztal Glacier ski area with a big mountain railway in a tunnel.

The snout of the Taschach Glacier, with the Taschach ice face above it.
The beautiful, rounded snow summit is the Petersenspitze. ▷

Hut Base Taschachhaus (2432m, DAV Frankfurt Section, 125 beds ☎ 05413 8239).

Other Peaks Bliggspitze (3454m) via the Bliggschartl, 3 hrs climb.

Hut Climb From the Mittelberg Hotel, ascend the Taschachtal on a vehicle track, then on a footpath across the slopes on the right of the stream to the hut, which lies on a grassy ridge below the Pitztaler Urkund.

Petersen Route to the Wildspitze Climb the ridge above the hut for a short way, then go up steep slopes on the left. Where the path branches higher up, turn right round a corner and continue as far as possible over the boulder slopes. Once on the glacier, keep to its right hand edge (crevasses) and climb energetically to the Urkundsattel (3060m). Continue over the now gentle glacier slopes to the Taschachjoch (3236m). Staying on the northern side of the dividing ridge, traverse eastwards across the snow near the ridge. Then ascend the prominent ridge to the Taschach-Hochjoch and climb a beautiful snow arête to the top of the Petersenspitze (3482m). On the other

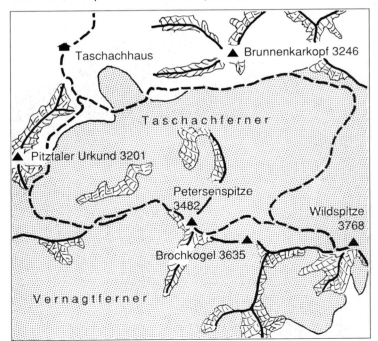

side, descend easily over the broad snow slope, contouring around the northern side of the Hinterer Brochkogel, and up a broad track over a steeper step with crevasses to the South-West col on the Wildspitze. Climb the ridge to the summit, sometimes easy step-kicking, sometimes unpleasantly icy.

Descent The fastest way down is by descending from the Mitterkarjoch to the Breslauer Hut and from there down to Vent. However, this would mean a very awkward return to the Pitztal or, more usefully, a traverse to the Vernagt Hut for further climbs in the centre of the range. Pitztal is best reached by descending the broken Taschach Glacier as far as the Mittelbergjoch where one has a choice of going back to the Taschachhaus, or crossing the col to the Mittelberg Glacier and descending to the valley on the mountain railway or on foot.

Sun-drenched glacier slopes between the Urkundsattel and the Taschachjoch. Beyond, almost obscuring one another, are the Petersenspitze (left), Hinterer Brochkogel and Wildspitze.

Fluchtkogel, 3497m

To travel up the Kaunertal (from Landeck) to the Fluchtkogel in the heart of the Ötztal Alps seems at first glance rather absurd as this peak and its neighbours are usually climbed from Vent. But that is just habit and at the same time proof of how silly people can be. The route over the Gepatsch Glacier, the biggest in Tirol, is truly an impressive experience, and one should spend at least one night in the highest hut of all, the isolated Brandenburger Haus (3274m). To witness the sunrise and sunset amidst the vast, eternal glacier world is something rather special.

First Ascent V. Kaltdorf, F. Senn and J. Scholtz with A. Ennemoser and G. Sprechtenhauser, 1869.

Character and Demands F An impressive route across vast glacier slopes with big crevasses. Settled weather is imperative, as one can get hopelessly lost on these broad expanses. The summit section is relatively easy, although the partly knife-edged North Ridge is substantially more demanding.

Timings Gepatsch to the Brandenburger Haus 5½ hrs, to the summit 50 mins.

Best Maps AV-Karte, 1:25,000 Sheet 30/2 *Ötztal Alps Weisskugel*; Österreichische Karte, 1:50,000 Sheet 172 *Weisskugel*.

Approach From Landeck in the Inn Valley go to Prutz and then up the Kaunertal to the southern end of the Gepatsch-Stausee (1900m, 43km, toll road).

Starting Point The Gepatschhaus (1925m, DAV Frankfurt Section, 80 beds ☎ 05475 215).

Hut Base Brandenburger Haus (3274m, DAV Berlin Section, 100 beds ☎ 05254 8108), situated at the foot of the Dahmannspitze, surrounded by glaciers on three sides.

Hut Climb The climb starts where the road to the Weisssee Glacier turns off to the right. Ascend the valley east of the stream for a few minutes, then traverse the steep slopes on the left for a long way along a terrace with a fascinating view down to the snout of the Gepatsch Glacier. At the end of the terrace, descend to the glacier and cross it diagonally, gaining a 100m height, to the opposite bank, where a boulder (snow) basin opens up on the right. Cross this to the small Rauhekopf Hut (2731m, open but without warden, 34 beds). Ascend to the glacier which is reached again at a height of 2840m. Now climb fairly easily southwards across the seemingly endless slopes (crevasses), before turning more to the left. Finally, pass the rocks of the Dahmannspitze heading due east to reach the Brandenburger Haus.

Summit Climb From the hut, traverse the uppermost flat basin of the Kesselwand Glacier north-eastwards to the Obere Guslarjoch (the cleft directly at the foot of the summit block, and quickly ascend the steep ice bulge to the highest point of the Fluchtkogel.

Traverse The mountain can be traversed following the exposed snow arête north-eastwards to a bend in the ridge, then descend (sometimes a snow-free block ridge) rather steeply to the Gepatschjoch (3241m) where one can make an optional detour to climb the Hochvernagtspitze (3535m) in about 1½ hours. From the col, descend a short step westwards to the glacier. Keeping to the left, near the steep slopes of the Fluchtkogel, descend the main stream of the Gepatsch Glacier westwards (many big crevasses) to the rocks of the Rauher Kopf. Then return the way you came up.

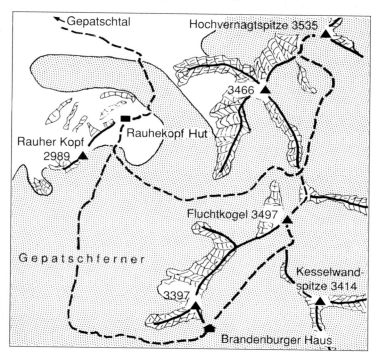

Weisskugel, 3738m

The peaks of the Wildspitze and Weisskugel rise very distinctly above their surroundings in the north-east and south-west of the Ötztal Alps respectively. Both are famous, yet the former is climbed by perhaps three or four times as many people as the latter, a fact only due in part to the less favourable approaches and the seeming isolation of the Weisskugel. The main reason is ignorance of the most interesting routes. In the summer, anyone who makes the 7km trek from the Hochjoch-Hospiz over the Hintereis Glacier to the Weisskugel has, by the evening, an indelible impression of the concept of 'glacier trudging'. Another long approach, and with little height gain, is from the north-east across the Gepatsch Glacier from the Brandenberger Haus – convenient for those already installed there for the Fluchtkogel. Much shorter and with more variety is the route from the south-east starting at the Schöne Aussicht hotel and using the Steinschlagjoch.

Since 1988 the Holler Hut on the southern side of the Weiss-kugel is available once more, though now called the Oberettes Hut (2670m, AV South Tirol, 75 beds). This is now the most direct way up the Weisskugel from the Matschertal.

However it is the northerly glacier ascent from the Langtaufer side which deserves five stars. Even though it is also a long route, it offers such splendid ice scenery, that no one can get bored. For example, there is the 200m high icefall on the faces of the Vernagl and from here the Weisskugel shows its most beautiful side. Like a steep, rocky snow pyramid of regular form, it soars some 300m out of the glacier basin – an imposing sight!

First Ascent J. Sprecht with J. Raffeiner and L. Klotz, 1861; East Ridge Dr. Harpprecht and P. Dangl.

Character and Demands PD–/PD A big glacier route with many flat sections and crevasse zones, with a mostly easy summit ridge but exposed at the top. Or there is a direct route from the Weisskugeljoch up a steep, exposed rock and snow rib (East Ridge, II).

Timings Melag to the Weisskugel Hut 2 hrs, ascent 4½ hrs.

Best Maps AV-Karte, 1:25,000 Sheet 30/2 *Ötztal Alps Weisskugel*; or Österreichische Karte, 1:50,000 Sheet 172.

Approach From Landeck, take the Merano/Stelvio Pass road to beyond the Italian frontier on the Reschen Pass. In Graun

(Curon Venosta), turn off the main road and follow the Langtaufertal (Val Lunga) to the road end at Melag (10km from Graun).

Valley Base Melag (1898m), the last picturesque village in the Langtaufer valley, with hotels and a beautiful view of the ice peaks.

Hut Base Weisskugel Hut or Rifugio Pius XI Alla Palla Bianca (2542m, CAI, 45 Beds ☎ 0473 83191) situated in a unique position for viewing the big ice peaks around the Weisskugel.

Hut Climb From Melag, walk along the almost flat valley pastures for about 2km. Now ascend the steep slopes in long zig-zags to a corner, then continue slanting up the valley across the boulder fields to the hut.

Weisskugel, Weisskugeljoch (left) and Langtauferer Glacier from the north.

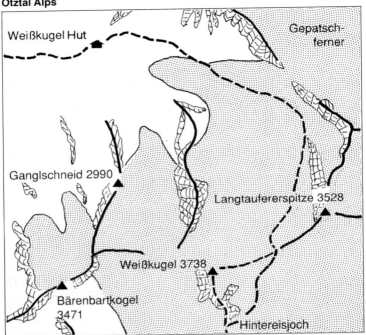

Summit Climb via the Hintereisjoch Cross the little moraine valley beyond the hut, then descend quickly to the Langtauferer Glacier. Traverse this eastwards, mostly on the flat, and keeping to the left side all the time. Then gradually turn southwards and continue below the beautiful but dangerous ice faces of the Langtaufererspitze to the Weisskugeljoch (3356m, crevasses). Cross this col and traverse the slopes of the Hintereis Glacier, climbing a short step on the way, to below the Hintereisjoch. Climb steeply up to the col (3460m), then up the snow ridge, steep at first, then broad and flat, to the South Peak and across an exposed rock section to the highest point.

East Ridge The direct ascent from the Weisskugeljoch up the East Ridge (II), a not very prominent rib, saves at least half an hour. In good conditions it is moderately difficult climbing over snow and blocks up to 3600m, then very steep and exposed direct to the summit.

Descent Descend by the ascent routes.

The North Face of the Similaun across the Marzell Glacier, with the ascent ridge on the right. ▷

Similaun, 3599m

This enormous ice dome is generally suitable for getting to know the high peaks of the Eastern Alps. Only 'generally', for in some years the final summit ridge is a knife-edge of bare ice. Then the ascent becomes an alarmingly exposed balancing act between the 350m high North-East Face and the even higher and steeper South-West Face. Anyone who climbs the short ridge on good snow and a broad well-trodden track will not be properly conscious of the danger but if you stumble here and slip, your moving companions on the (usually too slack) rope will never be able to hold you! The North-East Face was once a flawless picture-book ice wall, but these days a lot of horrible, grey-black rock islands show through it.

First Ascent B. Schlagintweit, with M. Raffeiner and J. Dumbner, 1847.
Character and Demands F+ A relatively straightforward high route, with few crevasses, but an exposed summit ridge.
Timings Hut climb 2 hrs, summit climb 3½ hrs.
Best Maps AV-Karte, 1:25,000 Sheet 30/1 *Ötztal Alps/Gurgl*; or Österreichische Karte, 1:50,000 Sheet 173 *Sölden*.

Approach / Valley Base See p75.
Hut Base Martin-Busch Hut (2501m, DAV Berlin Section, 125 beds ☎ 05254 8180), a classic mountaineers' base within reach of some twenty three-thousand metre peaks.

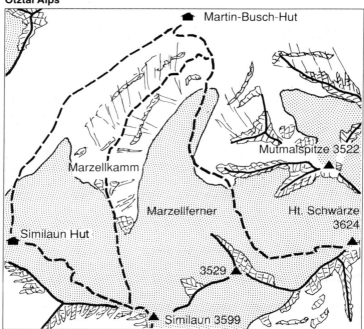

Hut Climb From Vent, follow the road southwards and cross the Niedertal stream beyond the last houses. Now follow the vehicle track up the valley on the slopes high above the stream.

Summit Climb Go a short distance up the valley beyond the hut then cross the stream and cut back left contouring round the end of the ridge to a fork in the track. Climb the upper path over grassy slopes to the Marzellkamm. Continue along the ridge, then also on the crumbly slope to the left, as far as the last rocky top (3149m). Now get on to the Niederjoch Glacier and climb it keeping well right of the edge to the summit ridge, finishing up the very sharp knife-edge to the summit cross.

Descent Return down the summit ridge, then descend westwards over the glacier and a small step to the Similaun Hut (3017m, private, 70 beds ☎ 05254 8119). Keeping to the left all the time, descend an arm of the here harmless Niederjoch Glacier to the boulder slopes and follow the path down the valley to the Martin-Busch-Hut.

Alternative Ascent It is possible to traverse the mountain east to west with an approach up the heavily crevassed Marzell Glacier (see p75) to gain the Similaun Joch (6-7 hours) at the base of the East Ridge.

Hintere Schwärze, 3624m

The principal peak in the eastern part of the Ötztal Alps has a truly elegant appearance. Its classy faces – ice to the north, rock to the south – form a sharp ridge. Thus from the Kleinleitenspitze the Hintere Schwärze appears as a fine, steep walled trihedral. However, for 'ordinary climbers' there is a very convenient glacier ramp on the western side, which can be followed effortlessly to within 100m of the summit. Only on the last bit does the exposure become apparent. Despite its great height and interesting glacier climb, the Hintere Schwärze is not as crowded as the Similaun.

First Ascent E. Pfeiffer with B. Klotz and J. Scheiber, 1867.
Character and Demands PD– A big and impressive high route, with crevasse zones and a steep, exposed summit block.
Timings A good 2 hrs to the hut, 4½ hrs to the summit.
Best Maps See p73.

Approach / Valley Base / Hut Base / Hut Climb See pp73/74.

Summit Climb A few minutes beyond the hut, cross the stream to the left and contour around the ridge to a fork in the track. Follow the lower path and then make a short descent to the snout of the Marzell Glacier. Ascend the often bare ice (crevasses) and cross to the east bank at a height of 2800m. Now climb up a steep boulder or snow slope to the upper, gentler floor of the glacier. Traverse obliquely across the glacier (crevasses) to the obvious ramp and ascend this to 3500m. Now turn left and climb the increasing gradient of the arching snow slope to the ridge and follow the exposed block knife-edge to the summit.
Descent Descend by the same route.

Overleaf: The Marzell Glacier and Hintere Schwärze with the glacier ramp clearly visible slanting up from the right. ▷

Fineilspitze, 3514m

Despite its lesser height, the Fineilspitze on the frontier ridge west of Similaun looks particularly elegant under full snow cover, with its northern ice face sculpting its north-east ridge into a truly flawless snow arête. The fastest way up is from the Grawand (cablecar from the Schnalstal in Italy), but here the more interesting north-eastern approach is described.

First Ascent F. Senn with C. Granbichler and J. Gstrein, 1865.
Character and Demands PD– (I). An easy glacier, narrow snow ridge and finally a rock ridge (often iced and hard).
Timings Hut to summit a good 3 hrs.
Best Map AV-Karte, 1:25,000 Sheet 30/2 *Ötztal Alps Weisskugel.*

Approach, Hut Base, Hut Climb etc. See pp73/74.
Summit Climb From the Martin-Busch Hut, ascend the valley keeping to the right of the stream. Above the glacier snout, ascend the moraine slopes obliquely, to reach the Niederjoch Glacier at 2930m. Now ascend a glacier bay westwards and then climb steeply up into the Hauslabjoch (3283m). Traverse to the start of the North-East Ridge and ascend the exposed snow knife-edge, finishing over the block ridge to the summit cross.
Descent Descend by the same route or, from the Hauslabjoch, cross the Hochjoch Glacier to the West Ridge of the Seikogel, where you meet up with the high-level path to the Hochjoch-Hospiz. [*Editor's Note:* Another alternative would be to descend the South-West Ridge (snow/ice and easy rocks) to the col 3375m and head north (crevasses!) to join the ascent route from Schöne Aussicht and either go there (for an ascent of the Weisskugel) or return to the valley by the Hochjoch route.]

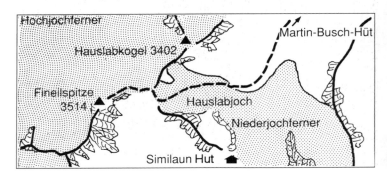

View from the north, looking from the Seikogel to the Fineilspitze and the ascent ridge; in the foreground are the ice slopes of the Hauslabkogel.

79

Schalfkogel, 3537m

A ski tour from the Hochwilde Haus to the Schalfkogel is frequently done. After an absolutely flat glacier crossing, there follows a rather steep 300m step. In the summer it looks easy enough, for the lower part of the steep glacier has melted and turned into a dirt slope; obviously not an elegant climb! However, the North Ridge with its fine snow knife-edge and classy glacier approach from the Ramol Haus does merit this attribute. Amazingly, few know this route, which is one of the most exciting and varied in the Ötztal Alps. Moreover, peakbaggers can traverse the Firmisanschneide without much additional effort.

First Ascent S. Ridge – F. Mercey, 1839; Firmisanschneide – F. Senn, Dr. Darmstadter with A. Klotz, 1870.

Character and Demands PD An attractive mountain route in the big style, with a glacier full of crevasses and narrow snow ridge.

Timings Hut climb 4 hrs, summit climb 3 hrs.

Best Maps AV-Karte, 1:25,000 Sheet 30/1 *Ötztal Alps Gurgl*; or Österreichische Karte, 1:50,000 Sheet 173 *Sölden*.

Approach Up the Ötztal to Obergurgl (1907m).

Valley Base Obergurgl (1907m), the highest Tirolean village with a church, nowadays almost entirely a hotel and guest-house settlement, with many lifts and cablecars and numerous possibilities for excursions (including day trips).

Hut Base Ramol Haus (3005m, DAV Hamburg Section, 65 beds ☎ 05256 223), situated on the steep slopes of the Spiegelkogel on a small rock pulpit, with a magnificent view.

Other Peaks Grosser Ramolkogel (3549m), a good 2 hrs.

Hut Climb In Obergurgl cross the Gurgler stream to the right and on the other side climb a step to a break in the terrain. Then slant upwards across the slopes for a long way to the south, to finish up a hairpin bend leading to the long since visible hut.

Schalfkogel North Ridge From the hut, traverse the boulder slopes southwards at a height of 3000m for 1km. Now climb up obliquely for about 100m to the glacier, which lies to the east of the Firmisanschneide. Traverse the glacier southwards, keeping above the biggest crevasses, to the distinct shoulder (3290m) on the ridge. Cross a small top to gain the Firmisanjoch (3287m).

Grosser and Kleiner Piz Buin above the Ochsental Glacier (Silvretta). ▷

The Dreiländerspitze from the north, with the ascent slope on the right; in the foreground the Jamtal Glacier (left) and the Vermunt Glacier (Silvretta).

An enormous glacier cave on the Morteratsch Glacier (Bernina Group).

At the Diavolezza (Bernina Group) with the Pers Glacier, Piz Cambrena and the East Peak of Piz Palü.

On the East Peak of Piz Palü with huge cornices on the left.

The Königspitze in the Ortler Group with its famous North Face.

Piz Kesch from the north, the principal Albula peak. ▷

Piz Bernina from the north-east with the Biancograt on the right.

rdwand.

l.

The Ortler from the north with the Upper Ortler Glacier, which the ordinary route follows; on the left the uppermost part of the North Face.

Outside the Payer Hut, the base for the usual route up the Ortler.

The summit ridge of Similaun in the Ötztal Alps.

The Schalfkogel seen from the Vorderer Diemkogel, with the North Ridge on the left (Ötztal Alps).

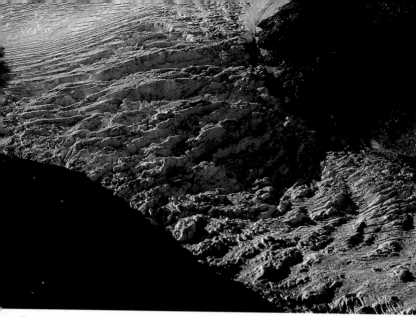

The Gepatsch Glacier at the height of the Rauhekopf Hut (Ötztal Alps).

◁ The Weisskugel and Hintereis Glacier from the Teufelsegg.

The Sulzenau Glacier and Wilder Pfaff in the heart of the Stubai Alps.

On the summit of the Hochfeiler, showing the East Ridge and North Face (Zillertal Alps).

The Olperer and Fussstein (the rock peak on the right) above the Wildlahnertal (Zillertal).

The ascent to the Schwarzenstein from the Berliner Hut (Zillertal).

Overleaf: The Grosser Löffler from the Schwarzenstein. ▷

The Rötspitze in the Venediger Group seen from the north-west.

A gigantic crevasse in the Venediger Group.

A view east past the Stubacher Sonnblick (right) to the Klockerin and the finely drawn ice peak of the Grosses Wiesbachhorn (Hohe Tauern).

Dawn light behind the Ankogel (left) and Hochalmspitze seen from the west (Hohe Tauern).

A protected path from the Hallstätter Glacier up the Dachstein.

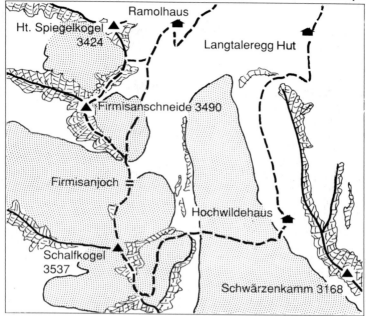

Now climb energetically up the rock and snow ridge to an intermediate top and up the very beautiful snow arête to the summit.

Traverse of the Firmisanschneide (3490m) Instead of the glacier work, one can cross this enormous rock peak (I/II) adding about 1 hours to the ascent time. Traverse boulder slopes south-westwards at a height of 3000m to just beyond the Spiegeljoch. Now ascend a ramp from left to right up to the notch (3251m). On broken rock, climb over a striking intermediate top to the summit and continue on the ridge to the aforementioned shoulder at 3290m (I/II).

Descent Descend the very bare South Ridge to the Schalfkogeljoch (3375m). From the col, turn eastwards and slant down to the right to a height of 3280m, then traverse the floor of the glacier northwards (crevasses) to its far bank. Descend about another 100m, then turn left on to bare ground. Descend very steep scree and broken ground to the Gurgler Glacier which is crossed directly to the Hochwilde Haus (2866m). Now you have a very long return walk past the Langtaleregg Hut (2430m, DAV) back to Obergurgl.

◁ *Crowds of climbers on the Gross Glockner.*

97

Hinterer Seelenkogel, 3470m

Which to include – Hohe Wilde (3480m) or Seelenkogel? The name Hohe Wilde is so well-known, its uppermost rock crest looks so striking and elegant, yet the trudge from the north to this peak is prolonged and almost flat. Conversely the Seelenkogel peaks offer sparkling, exciting and varied routes, which are only a few metres lower. Moreover, the name has nothing to do with the soul, but is taken from a small lake. The Planferner Hut (in Italy) stands on a rock pulpit at a height of 2979m, 'vertically' above the Pfelders valley, in an ideal spot to admire the sunrise. Thanks to its high location, it is possible to traverse two or even all three of the Seelenkogel peaks in one day.

First Ascent North-West Ridge – K. Edel and a party of six, 1871; Traverse of all 3 peaks – K. Meyer, J. Pixner, 1890.
Character and Demands The greatest obstacle on this route can be the crevasses, particularly on the Rotmoos Glacier. On the approach itself the ascent is up an easy block ridge, with a steep, exposed snow knife-edge on the traverse to the central peak. Not a suitable autumn climb on account of the crevasses.
Timings Hohe Mut to the Planferner Hut, at least 3 hrs; summit climb 1½ hrs.
Best Maps See p80.

Approach On good roads up the Ötztal to Zwieselstein, where you turn off left to Obergurgl.
Valley Base See p80.
Hut Base Planferner Hut (2979m, CAI, 100 beds ☎ 0473 85557), situated on a little rocky top at the foot of the Hinterer Seelenkogel in South Tirol.

Hut Climb From Obergurgl, take two chairlifts up to Hohe Mut (2653m). Descend the broad crest to the Mutsattel and continue on the ridge to a forking of the path (15 mins). Now traverse the grass and boulder slopes up the valley to the moraine of the Rotmoos Glacier, which is reached at a height of 2720m. Ascend the glacier in the direction of the Trinkerkogel and, at a height of about 2850m, gradually turn right between enormous transverse crevasses to reach the uppermost basin at the foot of the Scheiberkogel. Ascend to the Italian frontier at Rotmoosjoch (3055m). Descend in an arc across the Plan Glacier to the now visible hut.

The Rotmoos Glacier and Scheiberkogel. On the approach to the Rotmoosjoch, the glacier is traversed upwards from left to right.

Summit Climb From the hut, climb the block-like East Ridge directly to the summit (tracks and easy climbing).

Continuation to the Langtaleregg Hut Descend the very broad ice crest to the saddle (3335m) south-east of the Mittlerer Seelenkogel. From there it is possible to descend westwards down the narrow glacier, keeping to the right because of crevasses, or to ascend the block ridge (II) to the top of the Mittlerer Seelenkogel (3424m). Descend steeply following its elegant North Ridge to the saddle and either: move down the northern Seelen Glacier, swinging northwards in an arc down to the moraine valleys and (keeping to the right) then down to the path leading to the Langtaleregg Hut (2438m, DAV Karlsruhe Section ☎ 05256 233) or, continue up the South Ridge (II) of Vorderer Seelenkogel and cross the summit and descend north-east to the small but tricky Hangerer Glacier and down to Rotmoosjoch to join the Obergurgl path below the hut.

See following page for sketch-map of the Seelenkogel peaks. ▷

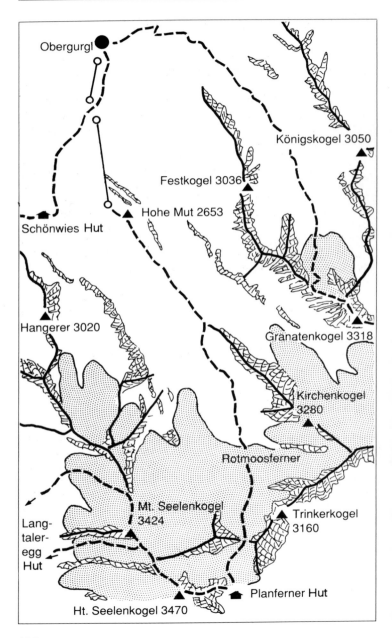

Obergurgl

Königskogel 3050

Festkogel 3036

Hohe Mut 2653

Schönwies Hut

Hangerer 3020

Granatenkogel 3318

Kirchenkogel 3280

Rotmoosferner

Mt. Seelenkogel 3424

Langtaler-egg Hut

Trinkerkogel 3160

Planferner Hut

Ht. Seelenkogel 3470

Granatenkogel, 3318m

Obergurgl offers a choice of three beautiful three-thousanders, which can be done as day tours. From the Hohe Mut, one can get to the Liebnerspitze (3399m), the north side of which is partly made up of wild ice cascades. The Hohe First (3405m) demands more ability because the Hochfirst Glacier finally becomes a real snow face 200m high. And the most elegant of all is the north-western aspect of the Granatenkogel. From this direction it appears as a symmetrical pyramid with a steep glacier, which unfortunately is heavily melted away in the vicinity of the summit. The route is most fun in the early summer, when snow covers the great amount of scree. Its name (Garnet Dome) is no accident, for the dark red gemstones are eagerly sought on its brown-red south-western faces. Incidentally, guidebooks always give the wrong height of 3303m for the Granatenkogel; the highest point is on the frontier crest 200m further to the south-east.

First Ascent A. von Worafka with P. Gstein, 1878.
Character and Demands A somewhat remote high route, with a small glacier full of crevasses, and a crumbly rock ridge which in early summer is partly a snow ridge.
Timings Obergurgl to the Granatenkogel 4½ hrs.
Best Maps See p80.

Approach / Valley Base See P80.
Hut Base None.

Summit Climb Start near the valley station of the Festkogel cablecar (no summer service) and ascend the steep slope in wide curves, then turn left into the narrow mouth of the Ferwalltal. Where the path forks, turn right and continue up the valley to the small Ferwall Glacier. Ascend the right hand branch steeply between the crevasse zones to the lowest notch. Climb the ridge – part scree, part snow – to the fore-summit and cross the knife-edge to the highest point. In good snow conditions, it is also possible to climb the very steep North-West Face.
Descent Descend by the same route.

Windacher Daunkogel, 3348m

The Sulztal is the central nerve of the south-western Stubai Alps. The Amberger Hut stands on a hump in the upper part of the valley. Due east the great rock faces of the Schrankogel (3497m) rise skywards above it, while to the south on the other side of the very broad, flat valley bottom there gleams a large glacier. This is the Sulztal Glacier, at the head of which stands the snow and rock peak Windacher Daunkogel. This mountain is little frequented unlike the only big rock peak on the glacier rim, the Wilden Leck (3359m). The long glacier climb from the north – past very beautiful icefalls – offers other benefits, such as a continuation to the south to climb its neighbour, the Waren-karseitenspitze (3347m) followed by a night at the Hochstubai Hut. This watchtower stands on the quite insignificant Wildkar-spitze at a height of 3174m, with an unobstructed view westwards, a perfect belvedere from which to watch the sunset!

First Ascent F. Jenewein and H. Buchner, 1878.
Character and Demands F/PD– A route up one of the big Stubai glaciers, with crevasse zones. The West Ridge is either a very sharp snow knife-edge or exposed climbing (II); substantially easier from the south.
Timings From Gries in the Sulztal to the Amberger Hut 2¼ hrs, to the summit 4-5 hrs.
Best Map AV-Karte, Stubai Alps, 1:25,000 Sheet 31/1 *Hochstubai*.

Approach Along the Ötztal to Längenfeld and from there on the very twisting mountain road to Gries in the Sulztal (5km from Längenfeld). Car park beyond the village.
Valley Base Gries in the Sulztal (1569m), once a very remote mountain village, now a popular holiday resort with a beautiful view of the Mutterberger Seespitze.
Hut Base Amberger Hut (2136m, DAV Amberg Section, 80 beds ☎ 05253 5605), situated at the end of the broad Sulze valley bottom, with many possibilities for excursions.
Other Peaks Schrankogel (3497m) which has a protected path up the South-West Ridge (4 hrs). The ascent is easy in ideal conditions but is often made more difficult by snow and ice – possible descent over the partly snowy East Ridge.

The Windacher Daunkogel across the Sulztal Glacier, with the West Ridge on the right. ▷

Hut Climb From the car park, walk up the flat valley bottom, then up the other side of the valley through picturesque woodland to the Vorder Sulztalalm (1898m, snack stop). Now climb much more strenuously up into the high mountains to the hut.

Windacher Daunkogel from the North Keep to the west of the stream and walk up the flat Sulze valley for almost 2km to its head. Climb up a little, then take the right hand fork in the path to a knoll with a beautiful view of the Sulztal Glacier. Continue southwards up the moraine steps to the glacier which is reached at a height of 2650m. Follow the right hand bank all the time passing two enormous icefalls on the left. From the upper glacier basin ascend pleasantly into the broad Wütenkarsattel (3103m). From here, there are two possibilities.

(a) West Ridge: Ascend the very broad snow ridge to the West Peak (3301m). Continue along an exposed rock arête (II) with little tops. Then traverse an almost level snow slope to the summit cross.

(b) South Face: From the Wütenkarsattel, descend southwards over scree to the Wütenkar Glacier and traverse left to the Warenkarscharte (3186m) Climb blocks and snow to the summit plateau and thence to the top.

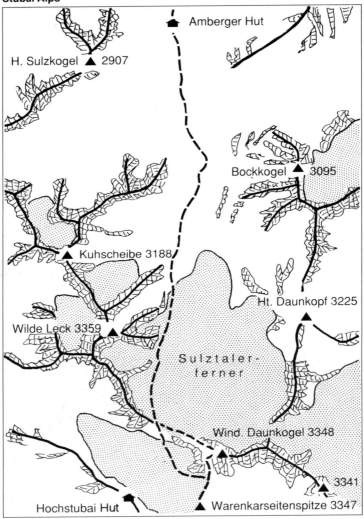

H. Sulzkogel ▲ 2907

Amberger Hut

Bockkogel ▲ 3095

Kuhscheibe 3188

Ht. Daunkopf 3225

Wilde Leck 3359 ▲

S u l z t a l e r -
f e r n e r

Wind. Daunkogel 3348

▲ 3341

Hochstubai Hut

▲ Warenkarseitenspitze 3347

Other Possibilities From the Warenkarscharte, climb the prominent snow and block ridge (I) to the Warenkarseitenspitze (3347m, 30 min).

Descent Either return to the Almberger Hut or from the col, traverse the Wutenkar Glacier for 20 mins to the Hochstubai Hut (3174m, DAV Dresden in Boblingen Section, 50 beds ☎ 05254 2414) from where a good track leads down to Solden.

Lisenser Fernerkogel, 3298m

In the Sellrain mountains, that dominate the northern part of the Stubai Alps, there is a string of really beautiful, rewarding glacier routes, such as the Längentaler Weisskogel (3217m) via the very crevassed Längental Glacier, the Hoher Seblaskogel (3235m) with its peculiarly narrow Grün-Tatzen Glacier, or the Gleirscher Fernerkogel (3189m), the principal peak standing above the Gleirschtal. However, the most striking shape is that of the Lisenser Fernerkogel, a symmetrical rock pyramid with 1000-metre slopes, which dominates the Lisens valley. Beyond this is a completely hidden broad glacier basin, the almost 4km long Lisenser Glacier, above which the peak rises only modestly.

The Fernerkogel is mainly coveted by ski tourers. Yet for many the dream has become a nightmare, for 1700 metres of height gain is hard work, especially since by early afternoon the snow is often already spoiled. The summer route from the Franz-

The 1000-metre faces of the Lisenser Fernerkogel plunge towards the Lisens Valley.

Senn Hut ranks amongst the more easy-going ascents (but not amongst the more agreeable!) for it is long and undramatic though best climbed in settled weather as route-finding on the broad glacier slopes is tricky in misty conditions.

First Ascent H. Buchner and F. Jenewein, 1876.
Character and Demands F+ A relatively easy high route, with an easy angled glaciers, and a nice block ridge (I) to the summit, only suitable for mist-free weather.
Timings Hut Climb 1½ hrs, and from there over the Rinnen-nieder to the summit 4 hrs.
Best Maps AV-Karte, Stubai Alps, 1:25,000 Sheet 31/2 *Sellrain*; or Österreichische Karte, 1:50,000 Sheet 147 *Axams*.

Approach From the Brenner autobahn. Ascend the Stubaital to Neustift. Turn right here and continue for 10km up the Oberbergtal to the road end near the Oberiss Hut (1742m).
Valley Base Neustift (993m), popular and lively holiday resort midway up the Stubaital.
Hut Base Franz-Senn Hut (2149m, OeAV Innsbruck Section, 260 beds ☎ 05226 2218), the biggest of the Stubai huts on a flat at the head of the Alpeinertal.
Other Peaks Rinnenspitze (3000m), which can be reached in 2¾ hrs on a path. There is also an exciting, and demanding glacier route up the Alpeiner Kräul Glacier to the Östliche Seespitze (3416m).

Hut Climb On a broad track between undergrowth, then across meadows to the hut.
Summit Climb Cross the stream by the hut and walk briefly northwards to the branching of the path. Turn left and continue up the steep slopes, then across the broad floor of the cirque to the beautiful Rinnensee, mirroring the surrounding peaks and their glaciers. Climb steeply upwards over scree into the narrow Rinnenieder (2899m), where one gets a view of the route ahead. Descend slightly and, scarcely making any height, traverse the Lisener Glacier. Then ascend parallel to the Plattige Wand to a height of 3000m. Climb a breach in the rock wall and then ascend the substantially steeper Rotgrat Glacier to the summit notch. Nice climbing up the block ridge to the summit cross.
Descent Descend the same way.

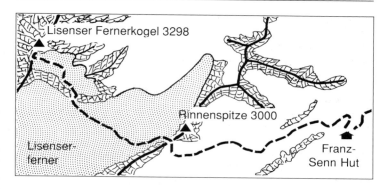

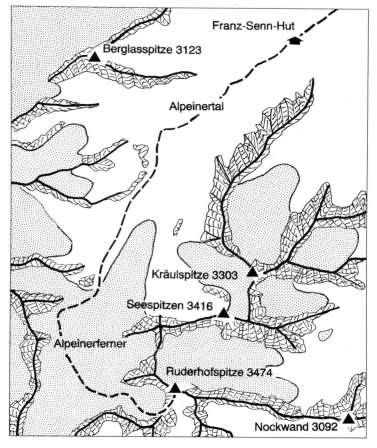

Ruderhofspitze, 3474m

In the central part of the Stubai Alps two peaks tower far above their surroundings, the Schrankogel (3497m) and the Ruderhofspitze. Whereas the former is conspicuously a rock peak, vast glacier slopes surround the latter, out of which it rises like a sharp horn. It is a long but interesting route from the Franz-Senn Hut up the Alpeiner Glacier, for there are repeatedly interesting views of the Seespitze peaks from the steep glacier and the great icefall left of the route, a fascinating, iridescent blue world.

First Ascent K. Bädecker, A. von Ruthner, P. Gleinser and A. Tanzer, 1864.
Character and Demands F+ A long mountain route over an extensive and crevassed glacier to one of the highest Stubai peaks, with an easy summit ridge in good conditions.
Timings Hut climb 1½ hrs, summit climb 5 hrs, long return journey.
Best Maps AV-Karte, Stubai Alps, 1:25,000 Sheet 31/1 *Hochstubai*; or Österreichische Karte, 1:50,000 Sheet 147 *Axams*.

Approach / Valley Base / Hut Base / Hut Climb See p106.
Ruderhofspitze from the West Continue up the flat valley bottom for 2km, then turn right on to the moraine and ascend it to the Alpeiner Glacier (2700m). Keep to the right up the glacier, past the big icefall, then traverse the flat basin, southwards at first, to beyond the crevasse zones, and finally eastwards into the obvious glacier bay under the Ruderhofspitze. Skirt below the long, arc-shaped summit ridge and get at it by a gully just south of the final summit pyramid. Continue up blocks and snow to the summit cross. [*Editor's Note:* The arcing southwest ridge can also be gained at P.3247m or at the lower Hölltalscharte. This provides an entertaining but easy scrambling rock ridge route to the summit.]
Descent By the same route (see map on p107).

The Wilder Freiger and glacier of the same name from the north.

Wilder Freiger, 3418m

Elegance is not the hallmark of the Wilder Freiger, which displays a broad and rather portly shape rising out of vast glacier slopes. Only on its northern side does it impress with its rather steep and badly broken ice slopes. Compared with the height of the peak, the ordinary route from the Nürnberger Hut is a beautiful but relatively easy climb but the round trip from the Sulzenau Hut offers considerably more variety, including mountain lakes.

First Ascent F. Leis and party, 1865.
Character and Demands F A relatively easy ascent, with a broken glacier on the way back.
Timings Hut climb 1¾ hrs, summit climb 4 hrs.
Best Maps AV-Karte, 1:25,000 Sheet 31/1 *Hochstubai*.

Approach From Neustift, ascend the Stubaital to just beyond the Grawa Alm (1590m, car park for Sulzenau Hut).
Valley Base Neustift (993m).
Hut Base Sulzenau Hut (2192m, DAV Leipzig, 150 beds ☎ 05226 2432).

Hut Climb Ascend through woodland and undergrowth to a shoulder on the Sulzegg, then up the bottom of the Sulzenautal. Then climb the steep slope on the right to the spanking new hut in a magnificent setting.
Summit Climb Traverse the rolling ground to the Grünausee. Pass it on the left and ascend a high cwm to the Seescharte (2762m). Now head south-west up boulder and snow terrain, keeping rather to the left of the edge, to a top on the ridge. Cross a short obvious knife-edge, then traverse the broad glacier, passing to the right of the Signalgipfel, and so up to the highest point.
Descent Possibilities From the Signalgipfel, descend the easy South Ridge for 100m, then turn right and traverse the uppermost snowfields of the Übeltal Glacier to the Müller Hut and down into the Pfaffennieder notch. Continue down the Fernerstube as described on p113.
Traverse of Zuckerhütl and Wilder Freiger The following 'Haute Route' is very worthwhile. Day 1: Stubai Glacier cablecar past the Dresdner Hut to Eisgrat to P.2870. Continue from here either by the route described on p112 or by Bildstockl Joch – Gaisskar Glacier (optional stop at the Hildesheimer Hut) – Pfaffenjoch – Pfaffensattel – Zuckerhütl – Wilder Pfaff / Müller Hut (or Becher Haus); Day 2: Wilder Freiger – Seescharte – Sulzenau Hut.

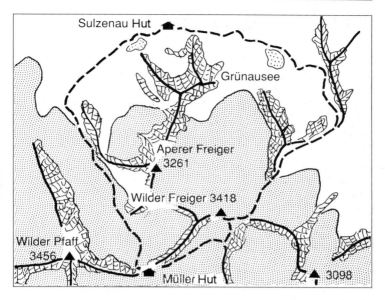

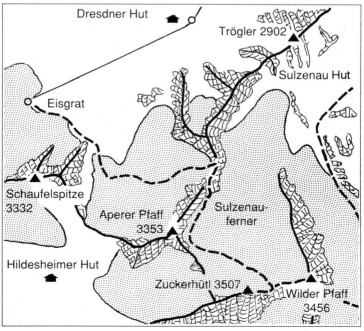

Zuckerhütl, 3507m

No other peak in the Stubai is known to so many climbers, no other attracts more crowds. It is rightly designated as the principal peak of the region, lying right at the back of the Stubaital with its conspicuous, gleaming mantle of ice. Moreover, its name (Sugarloaf) fits this glaciated cone perfectly. Only to the south does a high, dark rock face fall away out of view to the majority of climbers. The cablecars and lifts of the Stubai Glacier ski area have advanced ever closer to the Zuckerhütl. Its ascent has thus become a day trip and they come in droves. The steep, well-rounded East Ridge can be difficult if ice shows through in the summertime.

First Ascent A. Sprecht with A. Tanzer and another, 1862.
Character and Demands PD– A very popular high route, across broad crevassed glacier slopes, with a rather steep summit block of snow or ice, exposed in its upper part.
Timings By the shortest route, 2½ hrs.
Best Maps AV-Karte, Stubai Alps, 1:25,000 Sheet 31/1 *Hochstubai*; or Österreichische Karte, 1:50,000 Sheet 174 *Timmelsjoch*.

Approach Ascend the Stubaital to the Mutterberg Alm (1721m, cablecar, 46km).
Valley Base Neustift.
Hut Base Dresdner Hut (2306m, DAV Dresden Section, 200 beds ☎ 05226 8112), cablecar right to the door.
Other Peaks Schaufelspitze (3332m), one of the easiest three-thousanders, 1½ hrs from the cablecar.

Summit Climb Take the cabin cablecar to the 'Eisgrat' station (2870m). Descend slightly eastwards, then traverse the snow and boulder slopes at a height of 2800m to the Fernau Glacier. Now continue gently upwards and eastwards to below the Lange Pfaffennieder (3049m) and climb steeply up to its notch. Traverse a section of rock ridge, then a distinct ramp on to the Sulzenau Glacier. Continue southwards a short way, then south-eastwards over the flat glacier

Flattened by the 'worm's eye view', the North Face of the Zuckerhütl rises out of the uppermost floor of the Sulzenau Glacier. ▷

to the East Ridge above the Pfaffensattel. Climb the snow ridge, which is steep and exposed in its upper section, to the summit cross. If icy, the steep section can be avoided on the left over brittle rock (II).

Descent Variation Descend the East Ridge to the Pfaffensattel (3344m) and continue without difficulty over snow and blocks to the Wilder Pfaff (3456m). Descend its block-like East Ridge (I, belays), then traverse right of the ridge on the Übeltal Glacier to the Pfaffennieder (3136m, adjacent to the wardened CAI Müller Hut). Cross the col and descend a short steep step to the Fernerstube Glacier. Continue down the right hand side of this very crevassed glacier. Finally, follow a moraine path past the Blue Lake down to the Sulzenau Hut (see p110). [*Editor's Note:* It is also possible to traverse the Wilder Freiger *en route* to the Sulzenau Hut. See note on p110.]

Zillertal Alps

A relatively hard gneiss is responsible for the impressive scenery of the Zillertal Alps. The steep ridges are jagged knife-edges with pinnacles and angular towers. Likewise, the rock accounts for the special look of the region's glaciers. If one compares the 'Kees' of the Zillertal with the 'Ferner' of the Ötztal Alps, the difference in the crevasse patterns is obvious to the eye. On the northern side of the Zillertal peaks there is scarcely one icefield that is not wildly disrupted, waiting for you with impressive icefalls! The reason is the lie of the land underneath, for the glaciers have so far not managed to smooth away their floors or to scoop out round basins.

Such landscape makes the routes doubly demanding. Thus any climber going from the Greizer Hut to climb the Grosser Löffler or the Schwarzenstein, or even over the Waxeckkees to the Grosser Möseler, should be well experienced in dealing with crevasses and icefalls. Besides, there is a string of peaks which defend themselves with steep rocky rises requiring rock-climbing skills. Wildgerlosspitze is a peak of this sort, situated in the eastern part of the range (see p131). This is decorated with needle-like rock slabs. However, the most elegant peak in the entire range, the Turnerkamp (3420m), is not included here, being too hard for this guide. Its ascent from the north, from the Berlin Hut over the Hornkees, is amongst the more exacting climbs in this region (although easier from the Nöfesjoch Hut) and is a mixed high route with thrilling rock-climbing (III) up its West Ridge.

Other glacier routes include the Hohe Weisszint (3371m) on the crest east of the Hochfeiler, from either the new Hochfeiler Hut or the Eisbruggjoch Hut; and the Dritte Hornspitze (3254m), also called Berlinspitze, which can be climbed from the hut of the same name. Less well-known and less visited, on the other hand, is the area around the Kasseler Hut in the heart of the Stilluppe with the relatively easy Wollbachspitze (3210m) as the principal objective. On account of the numerous crevasses and steep steps, the lonely route over the Westliche Stilluppkees is much more demanding; the rock-climbing on the North-East Ridge of the Keilbachspitze (3093m, III) also requires ability.

Kuchelmooskees and Reichenspitze in the eastern Zillertal Alps. ▷

Olperer, 3476m

The Olperer is one of the most prominent peaks in the Eastern Alps, so naturally it is included in this guidebook. The peak is on the eastern side and one can be comfortably wafted aloft and then conquer this sharp-cut, elegant peak in a surprise attack. However, anyone who prefers a mountain route in the classic style chooses the westerly approach from the Valstal via the Geraer Hut, base for big and very demanding climbing on primary rocks, such as the North edge of Fussstein (V) a very beautiful route on firm slabs. [See *Extreme Alpine Rock* Chap 46] However, here we are concerned with the Olperer.

First Ascent A. von Bohm, E. and O. Zsigmondy, 1879.
Character and Demands PD– A short glacier approach, then climbing up a beautiful, very exposed, but well protected, slab ridge (II).
Timings Hut climb 2¾ hrs, summit climb 3½ hrs.
Best Maps AV-Karte, 1:25,000 Sheet 35/1 *Zillertal Alps West*; or Österreichische Karte, 1:50,000 Sheet 149 *Lanersbach*.

Approach From Innsbruck take the Brenner Pass road as far as St. Jodok, then turn east and go 8km up the scenically charming Valstal to Gasthaus Touristenrast (1345m).
Valley Base Vals (1271m), a straggly and unspoiled mountain village in a quiet valley with views of the Hohe Wand and Fussstein.
Hut Base Geraer Hut (2326m, DAV Landshut Section, 100 beds ☎ 05222 45575).

Hut Climb From the car park walk up the flat valley to beyond the Altereralm. Now turn off left and ascend numerous zigzags to the Ochsen Hut. Continue southwards, slanting up the slopes to the Geraer Hut.
Summit Climb Ascend north-eastwards over grassy slopes, to the edge of the Olperer Glacier at a height of 2800m, with the imposing slab walls of the Fussstein (3380m) on the right. Climb steeply up the glacier near the small Wildlahnergrat, and around an ice hump above a mighty icefall, to gain the glaciated Wildlahnerscharte (3254m) overlooking the ski pistes of the eastern slopes. Ascend on the right first of all on snow, then move left on to the slabby North Ridge, and follow this (exposed) to the towering summit.
Descent Descend by the same route.

The Easterly Approaches Those looking for a quick way up the mountain can start from Hintertux and take the chairlift to the station at 2600m. From here climb the Gefrorene-Wand Glacier to the Riepensattel and ascend the East Ridge to the summit, descending by the North Ridge.

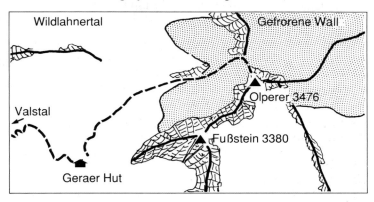

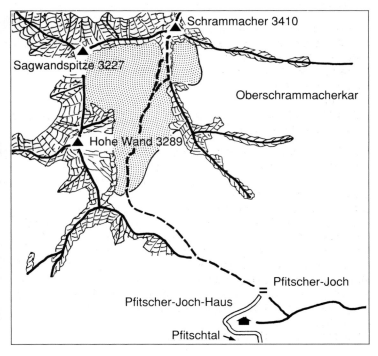

Schrammacher, 3410m

The north-western wing of the Zillertal Alps is also called the Tuxer Main Ridge. Here there are a few especially beautiful rock peaks with high walls and prominent edges, which pose attractive problems for climbers. One such peak is the Schrammacher situated at the south-east corner of the Valstal, near the Geraer Hut, from where it is seen as a dark, 700m precipice of really smooth cliffs with the classic North-West Pillar (TD–) as its most attractive route. Nevertheless, this mighty peak is relatively easily climbed from 'behind' and, thanks to the Pfitscher-Joch highway in Italy, which rises to a height of 2240m on its southern flank, it can be done on a day trip. The Stampflkees is one of the gentler Zillertal glaciers, although there are a few enormous crevasses. The South Ridge provides astonishingly easy block climbing, except for just below the summit where there is a section of real climbing. Anyone who loves being on rock will get on to the knife-edge at the Schrammacherscharte as the first prominent rock top offers climbing (III–) in the style of Mont Blanc granite.

Few ascents in the central Eastern Alps extend over such open terrain as here, so the views soon open up the most beautiful prospects. For example, looking directly on to the notorious hanging glaciers of the Hochfernerspitze, and not far away the Dolomites emerging above the mountains to the south.

First Ascent P. Thurwieser with J. Huber and G. Lechner, 1847.
Character and Demands PD– An easy glacier route in good conditions, then a block and slab ridge, which includes a steeper section (II+). The ascent of the entire South Ridge provides beautiful climbing to III–.
Timings From the pass road to the summit 4 hrs.
Best Map AV-Karte, 1:25,000 Sheet 35/1 *Zillertal Alps West.*

Approach From the north: Cross the Brenner Pass and from Sterzing head east up the peaceful and untouched Pfitschtal, the last part being on the rough but straightforward mountain road, to recross the Italian frontier at the Pfitscher-Joch (2246m, 32km from Sterzing).
Valley Base and Starting Point In the Pfitschtal there are only small villages and the last proper one is called St. Jakob (1449m), but at the top of the pass is a hut.
Hut Base Pfitscher-Joch Haus (2270m, ☎ 0472 60119), a mountain hotel on a small knoll in a magnificent position, with

picturesque scenery and little lakes all around.

Summit Climb At the lowest saddle, there is an indistinct path which starts up over the grassy frontier ridge. Ascend it, then gradually work more to the right up the extensive moraine slopes below the Grawandkogel to the start of the Stampfl Kees, which is gained on the far left. Climb straight up the broad glacier towards the summit, then work rather more to the right as far as the Obere Schrammacherscharte. Stay on the snow (big crevasses) and contour around the first obvious ridge top, then climb steeply up to the knife-edge. Climb straight up the edge, over a little wall on the right (II+), and so to the summit.

It is possible to ascend the ridge from the Obere Schrammacherscharte, in which case the cleft on the big ridge top is turned on its left hand side.

Descent Descend the same way.

Uppermost basin of the Stampfl Kees and the South Face of the Schrammacher.

Hochfeiler, 3509m

The spanking new Hochfeiler Hut (2710m, formerly the Wiener Hut) arose out of a real need. Now, once more, the highest peak in the Zillertal Alps can be climbed by its ordinary route without a mammoth march, in that one starts from 1700m on the Pfitscher-Joch road (3 hrs to the hut and 2½ hrs to the summit). In good conditions this glacier-free route has no difficulties, except right at the end where there is a short ice ridge. Moreover, it can be found without an exact description. For that reason the more varied approach from the Eisbruggjoch Hut is described here – the way that fell out of favour with the building of the new hut. An added advantage is that it can be combined with an ascent of Grosser Möseler (see p125).

First Ascent P. Grohmann with P. Fuchs and G. Samer, 1865.
Character and Demands F The route comprises many elements: approach to the col on a path, a climb up the crevassed glacier, and the high and partly steep southern slopes, with

finally a short, knife-edge snow ridge at the summit.
Timings To the Eisbruggjoch Hut 2 hrs, summit climb 4 hrs.
Best Map Österreichische Karte, 1:50,000 Sheet 176 *Muhlbach.*

Approach From the north, cross the Brenner into Italy and turn off the autostrada at Brixen to take the Lienz road to Brunico (Bruneck). Go north to Mühlen, then turn off left up the Mühlwaldertal, the last part being on a narrow, exposed mountain road to the Nöfessee (1856m, 30km from Bruneck).
Valley Base The Mühlwaldertal has few inhabitants, the highest village being the shabby Lappach (1439m).
Hut Base The Eisbruggjoch Hut (or Edelraute Hut) (2545m, CAI Brixen Section, 45 beds ☎ 0474 63230).

Hut Climb Follow the bank of the Nöfessee to the bay on its western side. Now follow the path left of the stream through woodland for a short way, then cross open meadows,

The northern faces of Hochfeiler and Hoher Weisszint (left) seen from across the Schlegeiskees.

and finally up a little valley to the hut in a rounded saddle. For a stroll after dinner, the little path up the Napfspitze (2888m, 50 mins.) is recommended for its impressive panorama.

Summit Climb Start off heading west, on almost level ground, and continue to a nearby ridge in the terrain, then slant up across the cirques to the Untere Weisszintscharte (2928m) for a surprising view of the Hochfeiler which from here looks rather broad and portly. Traverse northwards across the almost horizontal Glieder Glacier (crevasses), in order to reach the stony lower slopes of the Hochfeiler. On the first platform, climb fairly easily well to the left, to beyond the foot of the broad rock ridge. Before reaching the next line of rocks, ascend the mostly snow-covered, even glaciated slopes, on the right to the South-West Ridge. Climb the ridge to the summit cross, finishing up a narrow knife-edge.

Descent Descend the same way. Do not try to find a short-cut down the short walls of the South Face.

Additional Route The frontier ridge to the Hochfourspitze can be followed (PD+) but it is easier to cross the Weiserkar Glacier and reach it by its East Ridge (F+).

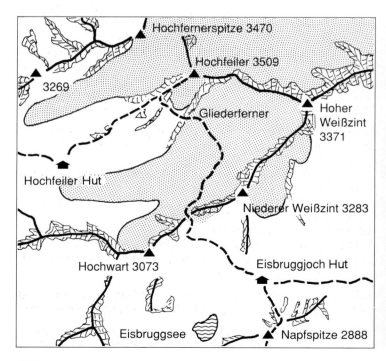

Grosser Möseler, 3480m

Because of its decidely fierce North-East Face, the Hochfeiler on the Austro-Italian frontier 'belongs' to the South Tiroleans, being almost exclusively climbed from their side. Thus the North Tiroleans regard the Grosser Möseler as their principal peak. It is an elegant mountain, which rises well above the glaciers which surround it. Understandably this objective is enticing for climbers. The easiest route from the north (described here) starts from the Furtschagl Haus and finishes spectacularly with an ice ridge and roof high above all the surrounding peaks. Even more splendid but also more demanding is the route across the Waxeckkees. This glacier above the Berliner Hut consists almost entirely of icefalls and crevasse zones! In addition, the peak boasts some fine rock and ice climbs. All of these climbs are demanding but there is a distinctly easier route from the South Tirol side, approached from the Nöfesjoch Hut (described briefly on p126).

First Ascent From the South – J. Fox, D. Freshfield, F. Tuckett with F. Devouassoud and P. Michel, 1865; From the North – W. Fickeis, F. Krischker with G. Samer, 1878.

Character and Demands PD– A climb up a very crevassed glacier, then a 200m rock spur, finishing on a beautiful snow ridge.

Timings Hut climb 2½ hrs, summit climb 4 hrs.

Best Map AV-Karte, 1:25,000 Sheet 35/1 *Zillertal Alps West.*

Approach Up the Zillertal to Ginzling and the Zemmtal to Breitlahner and thence by the toll road to the car park at the Schlegeissee reservoir (1782m).

Starting Point The Dominikus Hut (1805m, 25 beds ☎ 05286 216) at the northern corner of the Schlegeissee. This is a private mountain hotel with a very beautiful view across the water to the North Face of the Hochfeiler.

Hut Base The Furtschagl Haus (2293m, DAV Berlin Section, 110 beds), situated on the pastures high above the valley, with an especially imposing view of the broken Schlegeiskees and the Hochfeiler's 500m icy North Face.

Hut Climb Follow track along the bank of the Schlegeissee and the valley beyond. At a height of 1860m, ascend the very steep

Illustration on the following double page: The Grosser Möseler from the north-west, with (centre right) the foot of the ascent ridge rising out of the glacier. ▷

slopes on the left, with many zig-zags, to the start of the high cirque, from where the hut is soon reached.

Summit Climb From the hut, cross the stream southwards on to the moraine crest and ascend this for an hour to the edge of the glacier. Follow the mostly obvious track across the badly broken icefield of the Furtschaglkees to the striking West Spur of the Möseler. Start the climb in the big broken rock (snow) gully right of the lowest point and ascend the rock on its right hand side without difficulty to the upper snow ridge. Climb this, firstly up a knife-edge, then on a broad roof to the highest point.

Descent Descend the same way.

Grosser Möseler from the South F+ The South Tirolean side offers a climb with less difficulties (scarcely any crevasses). From the Nöfessee (see p121), ascend to the Nöfesjoch Hut (2407m, 1¾ hrs). Follow the high path to the East Nofes Glacier and either ascend this or go left of it, on grass, moraine and rock slopes to the uppermost glacier basin on the left. Climb more steeply to the East Ridge and up this to the summit. 3½ hrs from the hut.

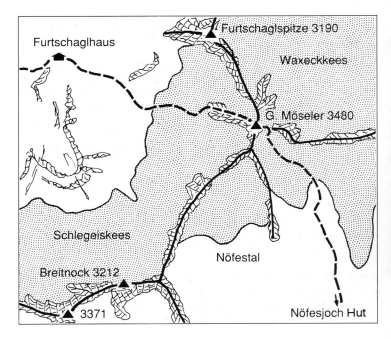

Schwarzenstein, 3369m

From the north, the Schwarzenstein appears (perversely) as a white ridge. That is why ski tourers also regard it as their favourite Zillertal peak. Starting from Whitsun, they can use the Berliner Hut, which has no guardian during the ski season. Of course this route can be done in about 4½ hrs in the summertime but then it becomes a bit of a trudge. On the other hand, the ascent over the Floitenkees from the Greizer Hut is exciting. This hut is where the most impressive route up the Grosser Löffler begins. There are few glaciers in the Tirol which are so broken! Not until one reaches the ridge does the terrain become gentle and easy-going, then it is an almost level snow slope up to the summit.

First Ascent L. von Barth, J. Daum, A. von Ruthner with G. Sauer, 1858.

Character and Demands PD— This is an especially exacting ice route because of the crevasses and icefalls of the Floitenkees. Easy in the summit area.

TimingsHut climb 3½ hrs, summit climb according to the state of the glacier 3-4 hrs.

Best Maps AV-Karte, 1:25,000 Sheet 35/2 *Zillertal Alps Central*; or Österreichische Karte, 1:50,000 Sheet 150 *Zell am Ziller*.

Approach / Valley Base / Hut Base / Hut Climb See p129.

Summit Climb Follow the lower of the two paths to the Floitenkees. No route description is necessary for the ascent of this. Generally speaking, one makes for the foot of the North Ridge of the Floitenspitze and passes to the right of it into the flat upper basin, which leads to the Tribbachsattel (3028m, Italian frontier). Traverse west then north-west around the Felskopfe to the summit plateau, and so to the summit, which barely rises above the level of the ice.

Descent Return by the same route or – much easier – to the Schwarzensteinsattel (optional 30 min. detour up the Grosser Mörchner) and then down the Schwarzensteinkees working round to the right lower down to the moraine path leading to the Berliner Hut (2042m, DAV Berlin Section, 150 beds ☎ 05286 223).

Alternative from the South The ascent to the Tribbachsattel can be made easily from the Schwarzenstein Hut in Italy which is linked to the Eisbruggjoch and Nöfesjoch Huts by the high-level Stabeler footpath (see pp121 and 126).

Grosser Löffler, 3379m

Even in a range like the Zillertal Alps, with its many prominent
peaks, the Grosser Löffler is something special. It rises mightily
above its neighbours, dominating both the Floiten and Stilluppe
valleys. From the latter it is seen as a beautiful, striking
pyramid, with a 600m North-East Face furrowed with ice
gullies, running up from the much riven Löfflerkees. The
Floitenkees on the western side, with its height gain of 1000
metres, is an even more fractured glacier.

The long approach to the Greizer Hut is worthwhile if both Löffler
and Schwarzenstein (see p127) are climbed. The routes are not
technically demanding in themselves, particulary if there is an
existing track through the crevasse zones. However, after
fresh snow when there is no track, many a climber has des-
pairingly wandered to and fro, trying to find the correct way

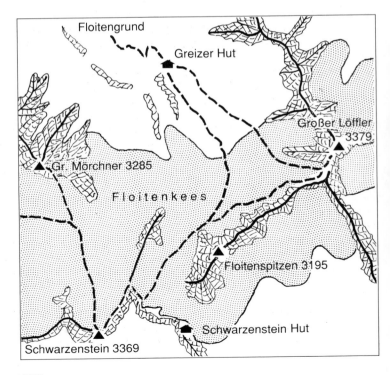

through. As the season progresses, crevasses open up even more. So for those who relish unravelling the teasing mazes of big glacier routes, the combination of these two peaks is highly recommended.

First Ascent M. Lipolt and party, c.1850.
Character and Demands PD– An ascent over a moderately steep, then short and sharp, glacier with numerous crevasses. Moderate block climbing on the summit section.
Timings Hut climb and summit climb 3½ hrs each.
Best Maps AV-Karte, 1:25,000 Sheet 235/2 *Zillertal Alps Central*; or Österreichische Karte, 1:50,000 Sheet 150 *Zell am Ziller*.

Approach From Mayrhofen to Ginzling, then 1.5km up the Floiten Valley to the Tristenbach Alm (1177m).
Valley Base Ginzling-Dornauberg (985m), a small holiday resort in a deep and narrow but nevertheless very picturesque valley.
Hut Base The Greizer Hut (2227m, DAV Greiz, 75 beds ☎ 0528 2234), situated high above the narrow Floiten valley, with fine views of the glacier and the rugged flank of the Mörchner.
Hut Climb From the car park, follow the vehicle track, then a footpath to the narrow Floiten valley where a path zig-zags up steep slopes on the left to the hut.
Summit Climb From the Greizer Hut, ascend the upper of the two paths, slanting across the slopes to the Floitenkees, which is reached at a height of about 2600m. Climb the broken ice slopes to the foot of the West Ridge of the Löffler. Pass to the right of this into the glacier bay beyond and climb (rather steeply in places) up to the top left hand corner. Ascend a steep block and snow slope on to the summit roof and ascend this to the highest point.
Descent Descend by the same route.
Continuation to the Schwarzenstein From the summit of the Löffler, descend to the glacier, and traverse left under the unimportant Tribbachspitze. Ascend the striking ice hump (P.3180 on the AV map) and on the other side descend to the Floitenkees via a short ice face. Contour around the two Floiten peaks on the north side – big crevasses – to the Tribbachsattel and continue as described on p127. 3½ hrs from summit to summit, a marvellous and demanding high route.

Reichenspitze, 3303m
Wildgerlosspitze, 3276m

Routes, which are rated amongst the most beautiful and interesting in the Zillertal, lead up the Reichenspitze on three sides. The Wildgerlostal, without doubt, offers the most impressive scenery with its boulders and glacier polished rocks, waterfalls, big mountain lakes and the very broken Wildgerloskees. But the Zillergrund approach is preferred because of Wildgerlosspitze, the roughest rock citadel in the entire Zillertal Alps, is best tackled from this side. On the East Ridge particularly there are some very exciting towers and slabs of rock with smooth, vertical faces. From there, the Reichenspitze, too, appears as an especially slender and elegant cone, which looks more rebuffing than it really is. It is only possible for fit climbers to do both peaks in one day from the Plauener Hut and one must be competent on steep rock of Grade II.

First Ascent P. Grohmann and party, 1866; V. Sieger with S. Kirchler, 1877.
Character and Demands F+/PD An approach over a short but badly broken glacier, and broken rocks to the summit, which is only unpleasant when icy. Climbing on the Wildgerlosspitze to II.
Timings Hut climb and summit climb, each 2¾ hrs; traverse to Wildgerlosspitze 2 hrs.
Best Maps AV-Karte, 1:25,000 Sheet 35/3 *Zillertal Alps East*; or Österreichische Karte, 1:50,000 Sheet 151 *Krimml*.

Approach From Mayrhofen head up the Zillergrund to Barenbad (1450m, 15km from the Mayrhofen).
Starting Point Hotel Bärenbad (1450m), the focal point of many excursions from the narrow Zillergrund.
Hut Base Plauener Hut (2373m, DAV Plauen-Vogtland Section, 70 beds ☎ 05285 3114), situated in a very beautiful open spot with a big mountain backdrop.

Hut Climb From Bärenbad, ascend the footpath to the dam (or take the bus). Follow the northern bank to about the middle of the reservoir to just beyond the Kuchelmoos stream, then turn left and zig-zag steeply to the Plauener Hut.
Summit climb Take the path in the direction of the Gamsscharte as far as the uppermost cirque at a height of 2600m.

Now follow a smaller path northwards to the edge of the Kuchelmooskees. Climb a step, then traverse the glacier slopes (crevasses) north-westwards to the upper floor of the glacier. Turn right here towards the notch, which is cut into the foot of the summit ridge of the Reichenspitze. Ascend a broken rock step on the right of the edge to the upper snowfield. Climb the last rise and follow the ridge on its right hand side, climbing easily over blocks to the summit.

Descent Descend by the same route.

Wildgerlosspitze From the upper basin of the Kuchelmooskees, turn left into the notch at the foot of the South Ridge (3116m). Lovely climbing up the sharp edge to the narrow double summit (II, 1 hr from the glacier basin).

Kuchelmooskopf (3221m) This equally huge peak offers a distinctly easier alternative to the Wildgerlosspitze. From the notch described above (which may suitably be called the Kuchelmoosscharte), turn left and ascend snow and rock to the southwards-jutting summit. Impressive view of the surroundings of the Kuchelmooskees.

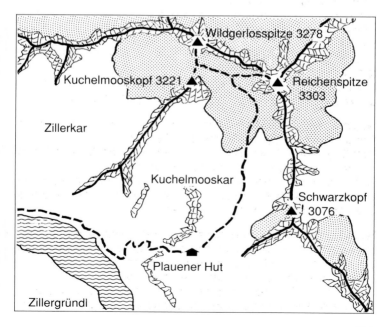

Hohe Tauern

Compared with the cohesive nature of the Ötztal Alps, the Hohe Tauern consists of a number of loose-knit isolated groups each with its own character and appearance. However, they could be grouped into two main sections divided neatly by the Mittersil/Lienz road running North/South across the range with the largest glacier massifs of Gross Venediger to the west and the Gross Glockner to the east. The Venediger Group is one of the most beautiful in the Eastern Alps, with its often demanding ice peaks offering faces and ridge routes. For anyone looking for further objectives in this area, there are the Malhamspitze 93373m), the Maurerkeesköpfe (3313m), the Grosse Geiger (3360m) or something demanding and striking like the Hohe Fürlegg (3244m), with an ascent over the Habachkees.

In the Glockner Group the glaciers are all concentrated around the Pasterze, or are connected to it via the notches in the main ridge. This phenomenon, now rare in the Eastern Alps, provides proof of the heavy glaciation of the region. Here, nine easy high peaks stand in a great semi-circle between the Johannisberg and the Fuscherkarkopf all easily reached from the Oberwalder Hut (2972m).

North of the extensive ice sheets of the Gross Glockner group is the scarcely less enthralling chain of peaks around Grosses Wiesbachhorn.

In the six other groups making up the Hohe Tauern, there are more beautiful big peaks, amongst which actually only a few like the Hochalmspitze are heavily glaciated. One of the more unusual mountains is the Hochgall (3435m) in South Tirol, with its demanding ordinary route from the north (climbing to II) being one of the big ridge routes, though it only briefly involves a glacier and is therefore omitted here. A similar situation obtains in the beautiful and rugged rock peaks of the Schober Group, where ice is confined to gullies and small basins, one exception being the Hochschober North Face. In the Granatspitze, Goldberg and Ankogel Groups, on the other hand, there are somewhat bigger glacier routes which are described in the following pages.

The Wiesbachhorn from the Hinterer Bratschenkopf, in a summer of little snowfall.
The ascent ridge is on the left, with the Wielingerscharte in the foreground. ▷

Rötspitze, 3496m

Although it has no striking, rugged faces, the Rötspitze is one of the truly elegant peaks. This symmetrical pyramid, of rock ribs and icefields, stands alone on the frontier crest where it turns to the south, between the Ahrntal in Italy (west) and Virgental in Austria (east), and towers far above its surroundings. Until recently scarcely anyone knew of this remote peak but recently it has become quite popular. Most people spend the night in the old and comfortable Lenkjöchl Hut, then plod up the Rötkees to reach this big, proud peak via its northern crest – the very ideal of a snow and rock knife-edge. Those who like ridges will do the whole ridge starting from the Vorderer Umbaltörl col, thus enjoying a climb of 2km with a 500m height gain – a real treat!

First Ascent A. and J. Berger and party, 1854.
Character and Demands PD– A mixed route, switching several times between rock and snow, on moderately steep ice and rock with some climbing (one section of II). The slaty rock, known here as bratschen, is unpleasant in icy conditions.
Timings Hut climb from Heiligengeist up the Windtal 2¾ hrs, from Kasern up the Röttal 3¼ hrs. Summit climb 2½ to 3 hrs.
Best Map AV-Karte, 1:25,000 Sheet 35/3 *Zillertal Alps East*.

Approach From Brunico (Italy), the main town in the Pustertal east of Brixen and the Brenner autostrada, head northwards up the Tauferertal and thence east up the Ahrntal to the Kasern, the last village in the valley, 36km from Brunico.
Valley Base Kasern (1595m). Starting point for two huts and several interesting peaks.
Hut Base The Lenkjöchl Hut (2589m, 55 beds ☎ 0474 64144) just above the col of the same name with an impressive view of the nearby icefields of the Rötspitze.
Hut Climb There are two possibilities. The shorter is the route from Heiligengeist up the Windtal, which is followed to the last

The Rötspitze, showing the face ascended, with, on the left, the white shoulder where one reaches the ridge. Far below is the Windtal. ▷

flat bottom before turning right to climb up to the hut. A longer but much more scenic and impressive track leads up the Röttal, at the head of which the Rötspitze towers up majestically. From Kasern, descend to the stream (or better still turn off right before the road climbs up to Kasern and cross the bridge) and climb steep, mostly wooded slopes to the upper valley. Continue up the almost flat valley bottom, and finally follow the left edge of the Rötkees up to the hut.

Summit Climb Exactly opposite the hut is a scree and rock spur running eastwards, cutting off the northern part of the Rötkees. Ascend this spur, then the glacier basin and the following somewhat steeper slope to the striking shoulder on the North Ridge. Ascend snow and rock to the

so-called Untere Rötspitze (3313m), an insignificant ridge top. Next traverse a snow basin, then ascend the slaty ridge (exposed in places), climbing the steepest section on the left up a chimney.

North Ridge from Umbaltörl From the hut, traverse north-eastwards to a corner. Then ascend scree and a short glacier snout to a basin which is ascended. At the head of the basin, climb steep slopes to the Vorderer Umbaltörl (2926m). Now stay on the ridge, which rises only slightly to start with, to meet up with the ordinary route at the shoulder.

Descent Descend over the shoulder and the Rötkees.

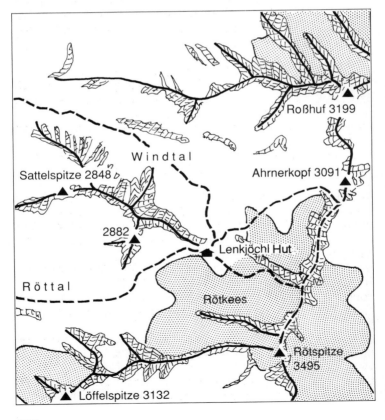

Dreiherrenspitze, 3499m

The Dreiherrenspitze is an 'impracticable' peak, for theoretically one has to visit three valleys in three different states. At the end of the Krimmler Tauerntal, which belongs to Salzburg, is the Warnsdorfer Hut. From there, one can gaze in wonder at (but only climb with great difficulty) the peak which appears as a black rock trapezium above the kilometre-wide and unusually broken glacier slopes of the Krimmlerkees. The peak looks entirely different from the Glockenkarkopf, which is reached from the Ahrntal in Italy. Rugged pinnacled, notched ridges and narrow, broken bands of snow rise to the steep summit. A really imposing sight! Yet most people naturally visit only the East Tirolean Virgental to climb the 'ordinary route' from the Essen-Rostocker Hut. If one is based in Italy, the peak can be climbed by an interesting, shorter but poorly glaciated alternative way from the Lenkjöchl Hut via the Hintere Umbaltörl.

First Ascent B. Ploner, M. Dorer, J. Feldner, 1866.
Character and Demands PD– A big glacier route with especially beautiful and extensive views. Dangerous in bad weather because of the complicated return journey.
Timings From Streden to the hut 2½ hrs, summit climb 4-5 hrs.
Best Maps AV-Karte, 1:25,000 Sheet 36 *Venediger Group*; or Österreichische Karte, 1:50,000 Sheet 151 *Krimml*.

Approach From Matrei in East Tirol (on the Felbertauern/ Lienz road) take the Virgental to Streden (1403m, 19km).
Valley Base Prägraten (1310m) is the centre in the upper Virgental which is very deep-set here between the steeply-rising peaks.
Hut Base The Essen-Rostocker Hut (2208m, DAV Essen and Rostock Section, 100 beds ☎ 04877 5208). This handsome double hut in the upper Maurertal opens up an unusually abundant selection of beautiful big peaks, though with comparatively long ascents.
Hut Climb From Streden, ascend the narrow, V-shaped valley on a pleasant path to a small floor, then climb up to the left to the hut.
Summit Climb From the hut, ascend the moraine path westwards for about 1 hour to the Simonykees. Traverse this

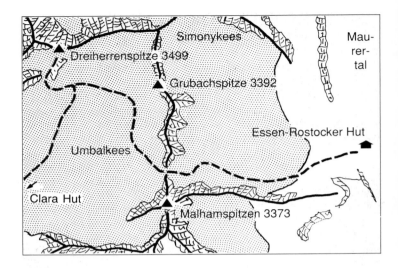

(crevasses) to the Reggentörl (3056m). Cross the gap on to the Umbalkees, climbing easily north-westwards, then head north to a broad break at 3150m above the icefalls on the left. Traverse westwards on the flat as far as possible, climb a small step, then get on to the distinct snow slope of the South Ridge of the Dreiherrenspitze. The steep step is climbed on the left up the rocky rib. Finally ascend the singular snow roof and a short, exposed ridge to the summit.

Descent Descend by the same route. For anyone who no longer has need of the Essen-Rostocker Hut, the best way back is down the Umbaltal to the small Clara Hut. After descending the 'small step', mentioned above, go down to the flat snout of the Umbalkees. Stay near the western bank and leave the ice to the right at a height of about 2500m. Descend the path coming from the unwardened Philipp-Reuter Hut down the valley to the Clara Hut (2038m, DAV Essen Section, 25 beds). Continue down the valley to Streden.

View of the Prettau Glacier and the Dreiherrenspitze from the north-west (from Birnlücken Hut)
with the snow ridge of the ordinary route in profile high on the right. ▷

Östliche Simonyspitze, 3488m

Anyone who loves glacier routes will find a real fool's paradise on the two equally high Simonyspitze peaks, which remind one a little of the Western Alps. The routes over the wildly disrupted Simonykees are decidely impressive, and require real experience of crevasse zones and steep snow slopes. Above all, the approach to the summit ridge of the Westliche Simonyspitze defends itself with icefalls and tranverse crevasses, and is much more pleasantly reached from 'behind', crossing the Reggentörl and climbing the Umbalkees to the Simonyschneide and the exposed connecting ridge. The same goes for the eastern peak: the glacier route is demanding and strongly dependent on conditions. The South-East Ridge is easier, more direct and clearer.

First Ascent T. Happrecht, J. Schnell, 1871.

Character and Demands PD A very interesting snow and rock ridge route from the south-east, full of promise, with steep sections. Or a big ice route over the broken glacier and the very steep areas below the summit. Very much subject to the prevailing conditions.

Timings 2½ hrs from Streden to the Essen-Rostocker Hut; from there about 4 hrs to the top.

Best Maps / Approach / Valley Base / Hut Base See p137.

Hut Climb See p137.

Ascent via the South-East Ridge Cross the moraine to the stream and briefly ascend the valley northwards. Where the path forks, turn left and climb more steeply to the Dellacher Keesflecken, vast slopes of glacier polished rock. Ascend these, increasingly on snow as far as a distinct ridge at a height of 2900m, which is flat at first. Then ascend steeply over rock with some climbing and the up snow. Continue up the elegant snow edge to the narrow summit, which falls away almost vertically northwards to the Krimmlerkees.

Via the Simonykees Follow the route described above to the Dellacher Keesflecken. At about 2700m, get on to the glacier and ascend it, winding your way through the crevasses towards the Westliche Simonyspitze. The icefalls above 3100m must be turned on the left. On the uppermost ramp, make an ascending traverse to the right below the walls of the main crest and finally climb very steeply (up to 45°) to the top part of the South-East Ridge.

Westliche Simonyspitze (3488m) Follow the route described on p138 to the Reggentörl and continue across the Umbalkees to the flat section at a height of 3150m. Now ascend directly north-eastwards and climb the steeper snow slopes on to the Simonyschneide (3440m). Continue up the exciting and exposed ridge (mixed snow and rock) to the western peak. A demanding route, sometimes with dangerous cornices; about 5 hours from the hut.

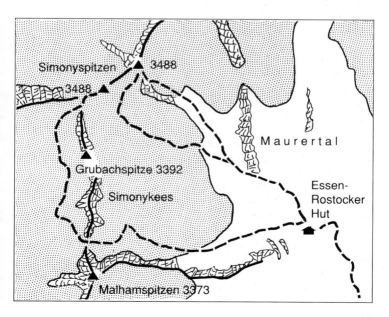

Gross Venediger, 3674m

This enormous snow-white pyramid catches the eye from practically every aspect. No wonder then that people were attracted to it early on. In 1828 Archduke Johann and fifteen supporters ascended the exceptionally broken Obersulzbach Glacier and the North-West Face to within 100m of the summit but the steep mixed terrain and rock-climbing to Grade III was too demanding for those days. In 1841, the forty-man party led by Anton von Ruthner was more successful, discovering the much easier route from the east.

Today the Venediger is still one of the most desirable objectives in this glacier region. Three huts with an overall capacity of some 350 beds are available for its ascent. Deep tracks lead in summer (and for spring skiing) up across the broad glacier slopes to the summit. The classic route is the one from the Kursinger Hut at the head of the Obersulzbach valley to the north-east. However, the five-hour hut climb and the endless broad, flat glacier bottoms

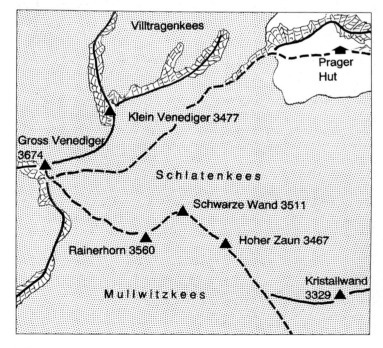

transform this route into a 'trudge', despite the splendid scenery. The described climb from the east from the Prager Hut is more dashing, for it offers the added attraction of a traverse of the Rainerhorn (3560m) and its satellites – one of the highest snow ridges in the Eastern Alps.

First Ascent A. von Ruthner with a large party, 1841.

Character and Demands F+ A glacier excursion, invariably on a well-beaten track, with dangerous crevasses and a steeper step on the summit block.

Timings From the Matreier Tauernhaus 3½ hrs, from Innergschlöss 3 hrs to the Hut; 3 hrs to the summit.

Best Maps AV-Karte, 1:25,000 Sheet 36 *Venediger Group*; or Österreichische Karte, 1:50,000 Sheet 152 *Matrei in Osttirol*.

Approach Either from the south, from Lienz, up the Isel valley to the Matreier Tauernhaus or to there from the north-east, through the Felbertauern tunnel (expensive toll road).

Starting Point The Matreier Tauernhaus (1512m), a hotel in the flat valley bottom, hemmed in by very steep slopes. It is possible to drive further (from 6am – 8.30am) to Innergschlöss (1691m, toll road).

Hut Base The new Prager Hut (2796m, DAV Prag in München Section, 100 beds ☎ 04875 6000). This hut is in a beautiful spot on the valley floor below the Kesselköpf peaks with a completely open view southwards on to the unusually rough icefalls of the Schlatenkees.

Hut Climb Follow the almost flat valley bottom from Innergschlöss, then ascend the steep slopes interspersed with rock parallel to the glacier snout up to the old Prager Hut (2489m). Finally, cross the rounded, glacier polished terrain to the new hut.

Summit Climb Continue to the start of the nearby glacier. Traverse south-westwards across the broad crevassed slopes of the Schlatenkees to the Oberer Keesboden. Ascend towards the summit, climb a step on the left to the ridge and another 50m or so to the highest point, which falls away almost vertically to the north.

The Rainerhorn Ridge Descend to the Oberer Keesboden and traverse south-eastwards to the Rainertörl, then all the way over snow to the Rainerhorn (3560m), the Schwarze Wand (3511m) and the Hoher Zaun (3467m). Finally, descend southwards to the Frosnitztörl and then eastwards to the Badener Hut (2608m, DAV, 4 hrs).

Sonnblick, 3088m, Granatspitze, 3086m

The big cablecar from Enzinger Boden to the Weisssee cuts the ascent of the Sonnblick down to a pleasure trip. This can be combined, without much effort, with the equally high and beautiful Granatspitze, with its dark pinnacles. Loneliness is definitely not a hallmark of this region. The 'Hotel' Rudolfs Hut was built as a centre for alpine courses, has 250 beds and some home comforts. Directly below it lies the large Weisssee reservoir, part of the Enzinger Boden barrage construction, which includes the 3km long Tauernmoossee. Beyond the Weisssee, the Sonnblick rises above gleaming glacier slopes which descend a long way. Ease of approach, lowly stature and a straightforward climb make this one of the easier objectives in this guidebook.

First Ascent Sonnblick – G. Demelius and party, 1871. Granatspitze – Surveyor and assistant, 1869.

Character and Demands F–/F+ An excursion over an easy glacier with some crevasses, then up a block and slab ridge (I) to the summit of the Sonnblick and, rather more demanding (I+ or II+), the Granatspitze.

Timings From hut to Sonnblick 2½ hrs, traverse to the Granatspitze 45 mins.

Best Maps AV-Karte, 1:25,000 Sheet 39 *Granatspitz Group*; or Österreichische Karte, 1:50,000 Sheet 153 *Gross Glockner*.

Approach Approaching from either Kitzbühel over the Thurn Pass, or Zell am See, turn off the approach road from Thurn Pass or Uttendorf and drive up the Stubachtal to Enzinger Boden (1468m) 17km from Uttendorf.

Starting Point Enzinger Boden (1468m) lies in the very narrow valley which is most notable for its power station constructions. The nearest proper town is Uttendorf.

Hut Base The Rudolfs Hut (2311m, OeAV alpine centre, 250 beds ☎ 06563 8221), with a beautiful open view. A cablecar runs up to the hut.

Hut Climb Take the cablecar or 2½ hrs on foot.

Sonnblick Ascent Descend to the eastern tip of the Weisssee (2250m) and take the right hand fork in the track along the little bottom below the Kalser Tauern. Turn right here and ascend into a snow basin and around a rock edge (protection) to the Sonnblickkees. Ascend the gentle snow slopes to the Granatscharte (2970m) and climb the block and slab ridge to the summit.

Traverse to Granatspitze Return to the col and either:

(a) climb directly up the North Ridge, which consists of enormous, dark-coloured blocks and prominent edges providing superb climbing (II+); or

(b) ascend obliquely south-eastwards below the rocks to reach the upper part of the East Ridge, which is climbed much more easily to the highest point.

Descent Descend the East Ridge and follow the usual route back to the hut.

Other Ascents Substantially more impressive are the peaks to the east, such as the Eiskögele (3434m) and the Johannisberg (3460m), with high faces falling away to the Ödenwinkelkees. The latter is the highest peak in the neighbourhood of the Rudolfs Hut. On the approach, the snout of the Ödenwinkelkees is traversed, then one climbs a small track up the extensive slopes of scree, broken rocks and snow to the Obere Ödenwinkelscharte (3228m), to reach the summit via the North Ridge (see also p153) after about four hours. From the notch, one can also climb the Hohe Riffl (3338m), a peak completely covered with ice.

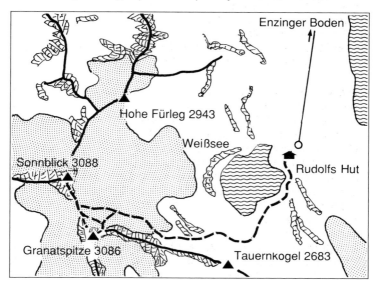

Grosses Wiesbachhorn, 3564m

This enormous ice trapezium lies far to the north of the main crest of the range and thus from this side catches the eye much more than the 200m higher Gross Glockner. The Grosses Wiesbachhorn is a very popular mountain and the Heinrich-Schweiger Haus (80 beds), on its western slopes is almost exclusively used for this ascent. Sadly, on the famous Kaindlgrat, the ice is retreating and the once flawless summit ridge is now dotted with rocks. However, combined with the high-level route from the Oberwalder Hut, it forms the climax of an impressive ice excursion. You are at a height of 3100-3400m all the way, crossing glaciers and five cols, climbing rock and snow ridges and traversing the bell-shaped Klockerin (3419m). Obviously a high-level route of this kind can only be undertaken in completely settled weather.

First Ascent Zanker and Zorner, c.1798.
Character and Demands F+ A narrow snow ridge (Kaindlgrat) and steep snow on the summit block, yet relatively easy in good conditions and with a track to follow. There is a broken glacier on the approach from Moserboden to the Oberwalder Hut followed by a high-level route without technical difficulties.
Timings To the Heinrich-Schweiger Haus 2 hrs, summit climb 2½ hrs. Moserboden to Oberwalder Hut 5 hrs, Oberwalder Hut to Wiesbachhorn 4½ to 5 hrs.
Best Maps AV-Karte, 1:25,000 Sheet 40 *Glockner Group*; or Österreichische Karte, 1:50,000 Sheet 153 *Gross Glockner*.

Approach From Zell am See to Kaprun and another 9km up the valley to the end of the public road.
Valley Base Kaprun (786m), a lively holiday centre with the summer ski area on the Kitzsteinhorn above it.
Hut Base Heinrich-Schweiger Hut (2802m, DAV München Section, 80 beds ☎ 06547 8662). The hut stands in the open on the steep slatey bratschen slopes on a knoll 'vertically' above the Moserbodensee.
Hut Climb From Kesselfall go by bus and goods hoist to Moserboden (2036m). The track starts beyond the eastern wall of the dam. Zig-zag up the very steep slopes to reach the hut quite quickly.

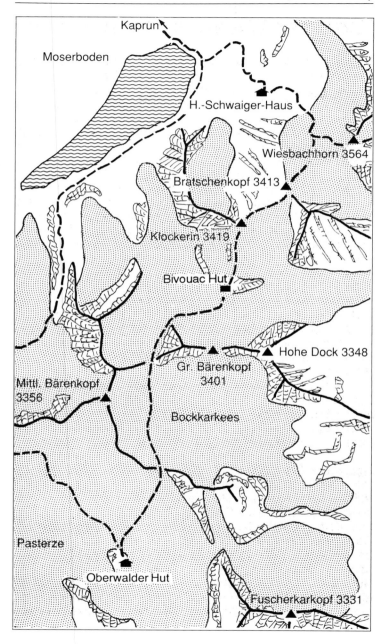

Ordinary Route Ascend the bratschen slopes and small rock steps (steel cables) to the ridge and the insignificant Oberer Fochezkopf (3159m). The Kaindlgrat begins here, an elegant snow edge which, nevertheless, soon changes to a broad and gentle terrain. There remains the very high and steep summit rise climbed partly on snow and eventually ice.

The Circuit from the Oberwalder Hut Walk along the eastern and southern banks of the Moserboden reservoir, then up the Bärenleite. At a height of 2570m, turn right on to the Karlingerkees. Continue south-westwards across the broken slopes to the broad glacier saddle of the Riffltor (3116m). Now traverse the flat snowfield south-eastwards to the Oberwalder Hut (2972m, mist-free weather essential!).

From the hut, proceed northwards to the broad Bockkarscharte and continue up steeper ground to the Keilscharte (3200m) between the Bärenköpf peaks. Cross the notch and descend the Bärenköpfkees until it is possible to traverse right to gain the Gruberscharte (3083m, somewhat above the Kurt Maix bivouac shelter). Climb the scree and snow ridge to the top of the Klockerin (3419m) and descend north-eastwards to a snow saddle. Continue upwards into the Bratschenkopfscharte and now either traverse the flank of the Hinterer Bratschenkopf (3413m) or climb right over it down to the Wielingerscharte at the foot of the Wiesbachhorn. Cross to the end of the Kaindlgrat and climb the peak by the ordinary route.

Kaindlgrat and summit of the Wiesbachhorn.

Gross Glockner, 3797m

Is there anything new one can say about the highest and most famous peak in Austria, this elegant, narrow rock knife-edge surrounded by big glaciers which rises so high above its surroundings? The resistant greenstone accounts for its precipitous shape and unusual height, with faces falling away 600m to the north!

The assault on this very unfriendly peak began in expedition-style in 1799. The Prince Bishop of Gurk, Count von Salm-Reifferscheid, was the 'spiritual' leader, while the brothers Klotz, two carpenters, distinguished themselves as mountaineers and were the first to reach the highest point. Beforehand, an early alpine hut had been erected at the foot of the Schwerteck Rocks (2800m), followed by another higher one on the Hohen-warte. During the successful ascent, sixty-two people were on the mountain!

Today the Glockner is one of the most climbed of the high peaks. From its foresummit, the Kleinglockner (3783m), a knife-edge runs to the main peak, a sort of narrow path (with steel cable), alarmingly exposed above the gigantic, smooth faces. In the mountaineering congestion, garnished with rope salad, many human dramas have been played out here. Time and again there are arguments as to who should anxiously grope his way forward first. For this reason, climbers switch over to an excellent alternative to the ordinary route – the Studlgrat with its beautiful firm rock (III). The usual ascent starts from the Franz-Josefs-Höhe at the end of the famous Gross Glockner Highway, with the traverse of the Pasterze, the biggest of the Tauern glaciers, more formally known as the Pasterzenkees. Anyone prepared to devote more time to this special peak and who prefers to get away from the crowds will greatly enjoy the following round trip: Wiener Höhenweg – Salm Hut – Hohenwart ascent to the Adlersruhe – return down the Hofmannskees.

First Ascent M. and S. Klotz, S. von Hohenwarth, Pfarrer, Horasch, J. Zopoth and others, 1800.

Character and Demands PD– A demanding high route which is frequently underestimated because of the milling crowds. It combines a glacier with crevasse zones, great height, an unusually exposed summit ridge and sometimes the hazards of hut congestion.

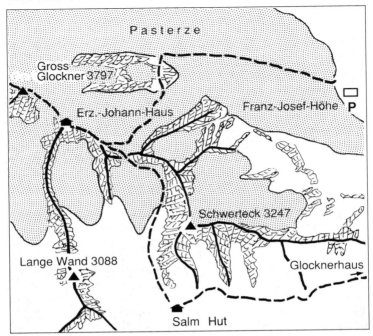

Timings From car park to Adlersruhe 4 hrs, to summit 1½ hrs.
Best Maps AV-Karte, 1:25,000 Sheet 40 *Glockner Group*; or
Österreichische Karte, 1:50,000 Sheet 153 *Gross Glockner*.

Approach By road from the north from the Pinzgau Valley and
Zell am See follow the Gross Glockner Highway to the Franz-
Josefs-Höhe (2362m, 48km from Bruck, toll road); from the
south up the Mölltal and through Heiligenblut.
Starting Point Franz-Josefs-Höhe (2362m) at the road end,
where there are two hotels and lower down the Glocknerhaus
(2136m, OeAV Klagenfurt Section, 82 beds ☎ 04824 2516).
30 minutes further to the Hofmanns Hut (2442m, OeAV Wien
Section, 70 beds ☎ 04824 2575).
Hut Base Erzherzog-Johann Hut (3454m, OAK, 200 beds
☎ 04872 5611), the 'highest' hut in Austria in a splendid setting
on the Adlersruhe.
Hut Climb From the last car park on the Franz-Josefs-Höhe,
descend to the glacier and ascend this diagonally, at first over

The Kleinglockner (left) and Gross Glockner with its North Face. ▷

ice which is later thickly covered with moraine debris. More or less opposite the Hofmanns Hut, on the southern side of the glacer, a distinct little path begins. Ascend for a fair way over scree, broken and easy rocks. Then ascend the crevassed Hofmannskees, steep in places, first southwards, then westwards to the Adlersruhe where stands the hut – the third highest in this guide.

Summit Climb Climb the broad ice hump of the Glocknerleitl, then rather steeply up to the rocks and on to the Kleinglockner (3783m). Descend the very exposed arête to the Glockner-scharte and climb slabby rocks to the summit cross. The fixed belays on this ticklish section are helpful but are often snowed up, which greatly increases the dangers.

Round trip From the Glocknerhaus, descend to the Margaritze reservoir and, on the far side, ascend to the Stockerscharte, then up the Wiener-Höhenweg to the Salm Hut (2638m, OeAV Wien Section, 60 beds, 2½ hrs). Ascend a path to the Hohenwart Glacier and a rock step to the Hohenwartscharte (3183m), then continue to the Adlersruhe (2¾ hrs from the hut), and thence to the top, returning by the Hofmannskees.

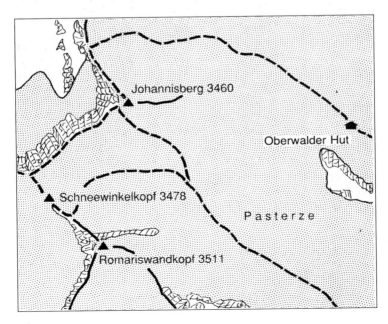

152

Johannisberg, 3460m

Seen from the south-east, the Johannisberg is one of the flawless ice peaks, yet does not look particularly striking. To the north, on the other hand, it drops away in a 250m ice face and to the west with an impressive rock wall. The approach from the Oberwalder Hut over the spacious and partly quite flat glacier is effortless, if a trifle boring. For that reason, one should either combine this with a descent via the glacier island of Kleiner Burgstall, which offers close views of the Teufelskampkees and Glocknerkees with the rugged peaks directly above or extend the itinerary to include the adjacent snowy peaks such as the Schneewinkelkopf.

First Ascent G. Bänerle and party, 1844.
Character and Demands F+ A high route over extensive glacier slopes with big crevasses, and a beautiful snow ridge.
Timings Approach to the Oberwalder Hut and from there to the summit, each about 2½ hrs.
Best Maps See p146.

Approach and Starting Poin See p149.
Hut Base Oberwalder Hut (2972m, OeAV Austria Wien Section, 110 beds ☎ 04824 2546) in a unique position amidst vast glaciers. Impressive view of the Gross Glockner!
Hut Climb From the Franz-Josefs-Höhe (2362m), take the broad track to the Hofmanns Hut and continue north-westwards across the slopes to the Sudliches Bockkarkees. Get on to the ice at about 2760m and traverse to the hut.
Summit Climb Traverse the very broad and mostly quite flat Rifflwinkel Glacier to the Obere Odenwinkelscharte. Now climb the snow ridge, steepening at the top, to the summit.
Descent Possibility Descend the South-West Ridge to the first shoulder. Then descend a glacier ramp in the direction of the Kleiner Burgstall, pass it well to the right and continue down the glacier to the Pasterze (badly broken in places, rather demanding).
Continuation to Schneewinkelkopf (3478m) PD. From the Johannisberg, it is possible to follow the ridge via the Untere Ödenwinkelscharte to the Eiskögele (3434m) and to continue over the Schneewinkelkopf to the Schneewinkelscharte. This takes about 3 hours with ice ridges almost in the style of the Western Alps, sections of climbing to II+, splendid and demanding.

Sonnblick, 3105m, Hocharn, 3254m

In the Goldberg Group of the Hohe Tauern the glaciers – as in some other regions – have visibly retreated. Moreover, climbers have 'lost' the Wurten Glacier, and with it the second highest peak in the region, the Schareck (3122m), which nowadays is a glacier ski area. So the principal objective remaining is the Sonnblick, one of the best known Tauern peaks. To the north it falls away in a high, dark rock face and steep ice, while the southern flank is harmless and, in part, strikingly flat but with two bigger glaciers. Above all, the hut already built by 1886 and the weather station on the summit contribute to the fame of the Sonnblick. The entire region was, nevertheless, famous in earlier centuries. Kolm-Saigurn, the starting point for today's route, was once the centre of a very prosperous gold mining operation. Today one comes across evidence of this activity in many places, such as spoil heaps and ruined buildings. Many place names like 'Goldberg Group' remind one of it too.

A very interesting and varied ridge route (with some protection) leads up the Sonnblick, as well as a route across the glacier with the singular name of Vogelmaier-Ochsenkar-Kees. Moreover, active climbers will make use of the high altitude Zittelhaus, in order to do the impressive traverse to the Hocharn. This broad and, seen from the east, somewhat shapeless ice peak is the main summit in the whole range. In good conditions it presents no serious difficulties but when icy the slatey bratschen rock can become unpleasant and even dangerous.

First Ascent Sonnblick – Unknown c.1700; Hocharn – J. Russegger, 1832.

Character and Demands PD– Easy climbing on the Sonnblick with belays on the ridge route, moderately steep and flat snow slopes on the glacier (crevasses). The traverse to the Hocharn is one of the large-scale high routes. Settled weather is therefore essential.

Timings Kolm-Saigurn to Neubau 1½ hrs, from there to the summit 3 hrs; traverse to the Hocharn 3½ hrs, descent from there to Kolm-Saigurn at least 2½ hours.

The view from the Sonnblick across the Vogelmaier-Ochsenkar Glacier to the Windischkopf and Alteck (on the left). ▷

Best Maps AV-Karte, 1:25,000 Sheet 42 *Sonnblick*; or Öster-reichische Karte, 1:50,000 Sheet 154 *Rauris*.

Approach Leave the main road between Zell am See and Bischofshofen at Taxenbach and follow the Rauriser Tal south-wards. Go right up the valley, finishing on a small mountain road at Kolm-Saigurn (30km).

Valley Base and Starting Point Rauris (948m), a popular holiday resort in winter and summer, is the only village in the valley. At the head of the valley, which was once wholly taken up with gold mining operations, are the Naturfreundehaus Kolm-Saigurn (1605m, 95 beds ☎ 06544 8103) and the Ammererhof (1628m, private, 48 beds ☎ 06544 6224).

Hut Bases Naturfreundehaus Neubau (2175m, 36 beds); and Zittelhaus (3105m, OeAV Rauris Section, 80 beds ☎ 06544 7143) on the summit of the Sonnblick.

Hut Climb The track starts behind Kolm-Saigurn and ascends quickly through undergrowth and glacier polished rocks to the Barbara Fall. Slant left to a small floor, where one turns off sharp right. Soon after, continue up through undergrowth, then cross the open slopes to the Neubau Hut.

The Ridgeway Continue up and down over the rolling terrain westwards to the big, flat valley bottom. On the opposite slope, first climb the steep zig-zags, then turn left to a ridge (this point can also be reached on the moraine path, which comes up from the east over slopes and a ridge). Descend into a small basin, then climb the snow or slab slopes to the wardened Rojacher Hut (2718m), a tiny old hut. Now continue along the very beautiful track on or near the ridge, which includes climbing some protected rock steps. Right at the end, traverse the flat glacier (big cornices on the right!) to the summit and the Zittelhaus.

Glacier Descent From the summit, descend due south across the Vogelmaier-Ochsenkar Kees (crevasses) to the Obere Brettscharte. Shortly before reaching it, turn eastwards down a steeper step and at 2700m make a level traverse to the left over to the Rojacher Hut, which is reached after a short climb. Continue as for the ridgeway. This route is only worthwhile when there is a reasonable amount of good snow.

Circular Trip to include Hocharn From the top of the Sonnblick, descend somewhat left of the ridge towards the Pilatusscharte (2905m). Continue across the Kleines Fleisskees, under the foot of the southern slopes of the Goldzechkopf, descending due west to a height of 2860m. Now traverse horizontally to a shoulder on the South-West Ridge of the Goldzechkopf. Traverse its really steep and, under snow, sometimes unpleasant western slopes to the Nordliche Goldzechscharte (2850m, with a path on the bare sections). This point can also be reached from the Pilatusscharte by a traverse of the Goldzechkopf (3042m), with some climbing on its prominent North Ridge.

From the col, follow the long snow and rock ridge to a prominent foresummit, with faces that fall away to the south and west. Then continue on the flat to the highest point of the Hocharn. Descend north-eastwards over the scree and snow crest, steep in places, to the Grieswies-Schwarzkogel, a completely insignificant corner on the ridge. Now descend quickly over snow just right of the crest. At 2800m, pick up a poorly marked path and work to the right across steep slopes to a fork in the track (2225m). Descend very steeply into the valley over grass slopes, broken rock steps and through undergrowth, before turning right back to Kolm-Saigurn.

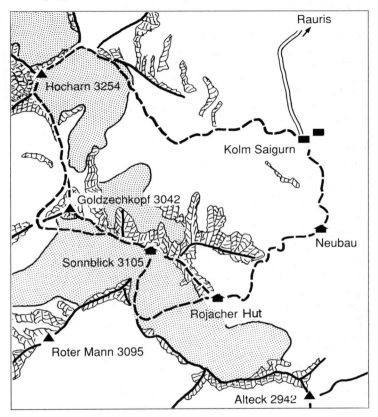

Hochalmspitze, 3360m

The Hochalmspitze rises as a broad pyramid above its surroundings. It is often called the last proper glacier peak in the Eastern Alps but actually the Dachstein lies further east. Three routes are frequently climbed, of which the Detmoldergrat with its protected rock sections offers the most excitement, while the Preimlscharte route (described here) is a real glacier route. The view of the North Face of the Grosselendkopf, which towers above the broken Grosselendkees, is particularly impressive! Anyone not tied to his car can traverse the peak southwards to the Giessener Hut and the Gossgrabe. There is also a special round trip of two to three days (see p161).

First Ascent P. Grohmann, 1859.
Character and Demands F+ A glacier route with steeper sections in its upper part, with crevasses, but without any particular difficulties in good conditions.
Timings Reservoir to hut 1¾ hrs, to summit 4 hrs.
Best Maps AV-Karte, 1:25,000 Sheet 44. *Hochalmspitze-Ankogel*; or Österreichische Karte, 1:50,000 Sheet 155 *Markt Hofgastein.*

Approach Leave the Tauern autobahn at the Gmünd in Kärnten exit. From there, ascend the scenically impressive Maltatal to the Kölnbrein reservoir (1910m, just 30km), with the Maltatal Sporthotel just above the dam.
Valley Base Malta (843m), straggly holiday resort in the broad, sunny Maltatal.
Hut Base Osnabrücker Hut (2022m, DAV Osnabrück Section, 65 beds ☎ 04733 351) situated on a small deep-lying valley floor in the 'Grosselend', with a beautiful view of the far off circle of peaks. Of the many mountains roundabout, only the Hochalmspitze and Ankogel are climbed frequently. Up above there are several interesting mountain lakes, such as the Brunnkarsee or the Plessnitzsee (2543m), which is passed if returning on the glacier.

Hut Climb Follow a vehicle track along the northern and western banks of the Kölnbreinsee to its southern tip and continue up the flat bottomed valley to the hut.
Summit Climb From the hut, climb quickly up the valley to the start of the moraine slopes. Ascent firstly on a moraine on the

left, then up a steep step, finally over a scree bottom to the edge of the glacier at about 2800m. Slant up to the right, cross the bergschrund and climb steeply to the Preimlscharte (2952m, unpleasant when icy). On the other side, continue up the stepped Hochalmkees (crevasses), climbing parallel to the ridge for a long time. Then slant across the slopes heading due south to the upper shoulder of the East Ridge. Then quickly up the ridge to the Schneeige Hochalmspitze (3346m) and over rocks to the highest point.

Descent Either return over the Preimlscharte to the Osnabrücker Hut, or descend the East Ridge to the notch at the Steinernen Mannin, go down a smooth rock step (steel cable) and the badly melted Trippkees to the Giessener Hut (2218m) followed by a long descent down the Gössgrabe.

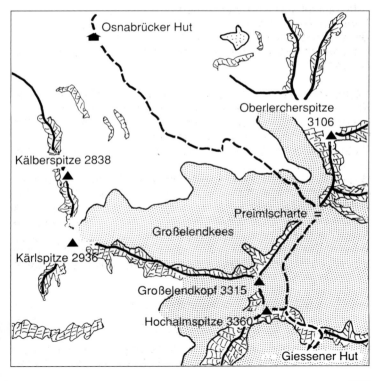

Ankogel, 3246m

The Ankogel has three contrasting sides. Dark rock predominates to the south, to the west an impressive rock and ice face falls away, and to the north-east the glacier reaches almost to the summit. This rolling and, in its upper part, even gentle Kleinelendkees then falls over a 400m high, badly ruptured step into the valley of the same name. However, the Ankogel does not really belong in this guidebook of glacier routes, for usually it is climbed from the mountain station of the Ankogel cablecar over a lengthy snow free route. It is only the following suggestion for a three-day round trip that makes it an especially attractive and alpine objective. Of course, the East Ridge climb from the Osnabrücker Hut, with the wildly foaming Fallbach, the mountain lakes and the open views of the scenic beauty is worth including.

The Ankogel is, moreover, the 'oldest glacier peak' in Austria. It was first ascended in 1762 and was climbed time and again in the early nineteenth century.

First Ascent Patsdig, 1762.
Character and Demands F– An easy climb from the Osnabrücker Hut (crevasses higher up), with a short but sharper summit ridge; moderate climbing (I+) on the ordinary route from the Ankogel cablecar.
Timings Reservoir to the Osnabrücker Hut 1¾ hrs, from there to the summit 4 hrs, from the cablecar 2 hrs.
Best Maps See p158.

Approach / Valley Base / Hut Base / Hut Climb See p158.
From Hut to Summit Beyond the hut, quickly ascend the Fallbach and its narrow valley, and finally a steep step to the Fallboden. Where the path forks, turn north over grass and scree slopes to the second fork, still some way from the Schwarzhorn lakes. Climb the upper path to the East Ridge of the Ankogel. Now either traverse the gentle glacier slopes (crevasses) on the right parallel to the ridge, or more on this knife-edge to the uppermost shoulder. Climb the narrow, exposed rock ridge to the summit.
From the Cablecar Go from Mallnitz by car or bus to the Ankogel cablecar and then up to the top station at 2626m (somewhat higher up is the Hannoverhaus, 2722m, DAV, 70 beds). First cross the slopes, then slant upwards over scree,

boulders and snow to the crest and up it to the Kleiner Ankogel (3097m). Now ascend climbers' tracks mostly on the right of the ridge, on rather exposed rock in places, to the summit.

Round Trip A three-day expedition through the range is worthwhile starting with the Mallnitz route to the Ankogel, descending to the Osnabrücker Hut and then continuing to the Hochalmspitze (described on p159). Now either descend past the Steinernen Mannin to the Giessener Hut (2203m, overnight there) or reach it – more demanding and interesting – by the protected climbing path over the Detmoldergrat and the Lassacher Winklscharte. On the third day, continue to the ridge at the Winkelscharte and over the Schneewinkelspitze (3015m) and Sauleck (3086m, protected climbing path) to the Arthur-von-Schmid Haus (2272m, DAV, about 5 hrs hut to hut). Descend to Mallnitz.

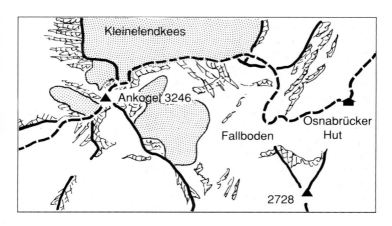

Limestone Glacier Peaks

The Dolomites can only come up with one real ice peak. Only the North Face of the Marmolata stands above a true glacier. Apart from that, there are a few ice-filled basins, such as that below Monte Cristallo, on Sorapis, on Antelao, on Monte Pelmo, etc. Also many of the deep-cut gorges are packed with snow, an aid in good condition but a dangerous obstacle when icy. The climatic differences in the Eastern Alps can be seen if one compares say the snow-free Cima della Vezzana, in the Pala group, with the snow-plastered Dreiländerspitze in the Silvretta – peaks of about the same height!

Somewhat bigger glaciers are to be found in the Brenta, on the Cima Brenta, on the Cima Tosa, where there is even an 800m ice gully, and on the Cima d'Ambiez. Yet despite the snow basins and ice fields, mountain excursions here never assume the character of glacier routes, although many a climber has been glad to have an ice axe, especially on cold days.

In the northern limestone Alps, snow and ice are more ornamental than significant in terms of mountaineering. Typical glacier characteristics are first apparent on the Höllental Glacier on the Zugspitze. Most striking, on the other hand, is the blue ice on the Hochkalter near Berchtesgaden. It is so protected in a steep north-facing cirque between very high walls, that it can sustain a mini-glacier a good 300m high. A phenomenom of a quite peculiar kind is the Übergossene Alm, a plateau glacier on the Hochkönig, whose once extensive mantle of ice is getting ever more threadbare and full of holes. What a shame! However, there is one real, large-scale glacier region in the northern limestone mountains – the central Dachstein Group. In particular, the Hallstätter Glacier has all the appropriate attributes, including many crevasses. The Gosau Glacier, with its big peaks, belongs to the picturesque. Amazingly, mountaineers do not take the limestone mountain glaciers as seriously as those in the central Eastern Alps. As if a fall into a crevasse on the Dachstein were less unpleasant than one, say, on the Zuckerhütl in the Stubai! It is absolutely essential to take full ice equipment for a route from the Simony Hut up the Hoher Dachstein.

The summit of the Hoher Dachstein above the Hallstätter Glacier (ordinary route). ▷

Marmolata di Penia, 3342m

Amongst all the mighty rock peaks the icefields of the Marmolata shine especially brightly. This multi-faceted Marmolata Glacier is very much one of the 'big boys', about 4km wide and descending more than 800m. From the north an ice peak of rounded form, the Marmolata falls away to the south in a long, rust-red and almost vertical flight of major walls and faces, much prized by good climbers. The contrasts could not be greater!

Only on the Marmolata is there such an ideal combination of rock-climbing and glacier travel. By taking the cablecar to the Pian dei Fiacconi, one can start a route at a height of 2626m, ascend mostly over snow to the Marmolata col, climb the well-known West Ridge and then follow the North Ridge and the glacier back to the cablecar. This gives a large-scale and relatively 'quick' round trip! The West Ridge is unusual for the Dolomites. While the edge falls almost vertically to the south, the north side is strikingly rounded by the action of once much bigger glaciers. Enormous, often scree-covered slabs, which drop steeply to the icefields, remind one a little of the central Eastern Alps. The protected climbing path also leads one across the rock slopes for a long way. This construction by the Nuremberg Section of the DAV dates from before the First World War.

First Ascent P. Grohmann with A. and F. Dimai, 1864.
Character and Demands F+ (from north)/PD– (West Ridge) A glacier route with crevasse zones and a much used protected climbing path of medium difficulty, rising some 250m or more, which should only be attempted in settled weather because of the altitude.
Timings Ascent from Pian dei Fiacconi over the Marmolata col 3½ hrs, direct ascent 1½ to 2 hrs.
Best Map Touring Club Italiano, 1:50,000 Sheet D56 *Val Gardena*.

Approach From Bolzano over the Karer Pass or from the Val Gardena (Grödnertal) over the Sella Pass to the Val di Fassa and from there on the good hairpin road to the Fedaja Pass (2053m) and a reservoir at the foot of the Marmolata, where there are some hotels.
Starting Point The southern bank of the Fedaja lake at the cablecar station.

Marmolata contrasts: ice to the north, high rock walls to the south. ▷

Hut Base Rifugio Pian dei Fiacconi alla Marmolata (2626m, private, 24 beds ☎ 0462 61368). Reached by cablecar.

The Climbing Path From Fiacconi, turn right (west) and climb up easily over snow and ice to a notch on the next rock rib. Descend from here a short way to the next, substantially steeper arm of the glacier. Turn right below the rocks, then ascend the snow bay to the notch of the Forcella Marmolata (2910m). This is the start of the protected climbing path (via ferrata) up the West Ridge. Most people come up from the south from the Contrin Hut. The well protected path, with steel cables, bolts, U-shaped cramps, footpaths and ladders, takes the left flank, crossing some large exposed slabs. The path finishes on the uppermost snow of the glacier, just 200m below the summit. Ascend snow easily to the top where there is a little refreshment hut.

Descent Descend the snow ridge (Schena del Mul or Muli-rücken) northwards, and continue over a prominent steep step, then down the right of the rock flank (I) to the glacier. Look out for the bergschrunds! Descend past crevasses and icefalls to the Pian dei Fiacconi.

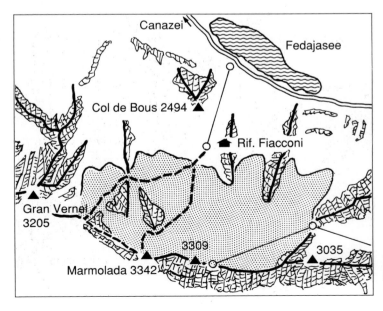

Hoher Dachstein, 2995m

The Dachstein is the last true glacier peak in the Eastern Alps. The two big icefields on this peak descend for 500m and 700m respectively! Their crevasses and icefalls would be genuinely impressive in the Stubai Alps, for example. However, the Dachstein has no need of such comparisons. With far-reaching, gleaming glacier slopes to the north, a kilometre wide wall to the south – this massif catches the eye from all directions and draws the crowds.

Those in a hurry use the cablecar from the Ramsau valley up to the Hunerkogel (2694m), then march across the uppermost glacier and climb gymnastically up one of the two protected paths up the ledges of the striking 200m high North-East Face to the summit cross. However, the approach from the Simony Hut over the very crevassed Hallstätter Glacier is one of the beautiful ice routes. If you want to see still more of this splendid range, the east-west traverse by a combination of the Linzer Weg and Dachstein traverse is a fine expedition (described here). For the return to Filzmoos the walkers' path under the southern walls of the Dachstein adds a spectacular finish.

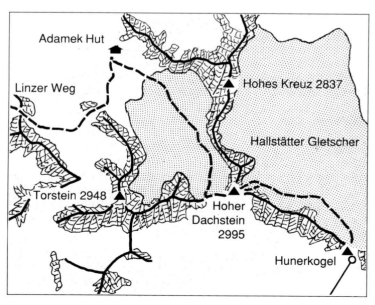

First Ascent P. Gappmeyer, 1832.

Character and Demands PD– An interesting glacier route and easy climbing (I).

Timings From the Hoferalm to the Adamek Hut 4½ hrs, to the summit 2¾ hrs.

Best Maps AV-Karte, 1:25,000 Sheet 14 *Dachstein Group*; or Österreichische Karte, 1:50,000 Sheet 126 *Radstadt* and 127 *Schladming*.

Approach Leave the Tauern autobahn at the Eben exit and drive 12km up the Fritzbachtal to Filzmoos.

Valley Base Filzmoos (1055m), a popular holiday resort with an impressive view of the Bischofsmütze (2459m).

Hut Base Adamek Hut (2196m, OeAV Vienna Section, 120 beds ☎ 06136 567), situated in a very beautiful spot just below the Gosau Glacier.

Approach via the Linzer Weg From Filzmoos, ascend the valley to the north to the Hoferalm (1268m, 5km, car parking). Now ascend the right hand stream to the Rinderfeld, where you pick up the Linzer Weg. (A still more beautiful variant is from Aualm to the Hofpürgl Hut and past the Bischofsmütze.) Now follow a very interesting section of the path with short rock steps and karst scenery, over the Reissgang to the Niederer and Hoher Hochkesseleck (2260m, impressive view, protection) followed by a 60m descent. Now cross scree and karst, then climb a steep rock step with aids to the Torsteineck (2258m). Finally traverse below the glacier and drop down to the hut.

Summit Climb Climb up to the Gosau Glacier and traverse the rolling icefield, firstly in the direction of the Steinerscharte, then southwards to the Obere Windlucke (2779m). Climb the protected West Ridge – to the right the South Face drops 700m – to the summit.

Return via the Hunerkogel Near the conspicuous gully (bolts, etc.), descend to just above the Hallstätter Glacier. Now either continue straight on down to the bergschrund, or turn right and traverse the face on a ledge and the rock path (well protected) to the snow. Carry on past the Dachsteinwarte Hut to the expensive cablecar and descend to the Ramsau valley or descend the footpath to the Pernerweg and follow this below the South Face back to Filzmoos.

Top: Looking back from the Linzer Weg towards the Hofpurgl Hut, the Bischofsmutze and the Armkarwand.

Bottom: Part of the South Face of the Dachstein, with the Hoher Dachstein (right) and the Mitterspitze. ▷

Peaks and Huts in Height Order

As this guidebook is concerned with the big peaks of the Eastern Alps, a few statistics on the theme 'The Highest' would not come amiss here. However, they only refer to those directly mentioned in the main text.

THE HIGHEST PEAKS

1	Piz Bernina	4049	Bernina
2	Bella Vista	3922	Bernina
3	Piz Palü	3905	Bernina
4	Ortler	3905	Ortler Group
5	Königspitze	3851	Ortler Group
6	Gross Glockner	3797	Hohe Tauern
7	Monte Cevedale	3769	Ortler Group
8	Wildspitze	3768	Ötztal Alps
9	Piz Morteratsch	3751	Bernina
10	Weisskugel	3738	Ötztal Alps
11	Palon de la Mare	3703	Ortler Group
12	Monte Disgrazia	3678	Bernina/Bregaglia
13	Punta San Matteo	3675	Ortler Group
14	Gross Venediger	3674	Hohe Tauern
15	Monte Vioz	3645	Ortler Group
16	Hintere Schwärze	3624	Ötztal Alps
17	Similaun	3599	Ötztal Alps
18	Grosses Wiesbachhorn	3564	Hohe Tauern
19	Rainerhorn	3560	Hohe Tauern
20	Cima Presanella	3558	Adamello Group
21	Monte Adamello	3554	Adamello Group
22	Piz Tschierva	3546	Bernina
23	Vertainspitze	3545	Ortler Group
24	Schalfkogel	3537	Ötztal Alps
25	Hochvernagtspitze	3535	Ötztal Alps
26	Hoher Angelus	3521	Ortler Group
27	Monte Mantello	3517	Ortler Group
28	Hochfeiler	3509	Zillertal Alps
29	Zuckerhütl	3507	Stubai Alps
30	Dreiherrenspitze	3499	Hohe Tauern
31	Fluchtkogel	3497	Ötztal Alps
32	Rötspitze	3496	Hohe Tauern
33	Firmisanschneide	3490	Ötztal Alps
34	Simonyspitze	3488	Hohe Tauern
35	Petersenspitze	3482	Ötztal Alps
36	Grosser Möseler	3480	Zillertal Alps

37	Olperer	3476	Zillertal Alps
38	Ruderhofspitze	3474	Stubai Alps
39	Hinterer Seelenkogel	3470	Ötztal Alps
40	Johannisberg	3460	Hohe Tauern
41	Wilder Pfaff	3456	Stubai Alps
42	Mittlerer Seelenkogel	3424	Ötztal Alps
43	Klockerin	3419	Hohe Tauern
44	Piz Kesch	3418	Albula Range
45	Wilder Freiger	3418	Stubai Alps
46	Bratschenkopf	3413	Hohe Tauern
47	Schrammacher	3410	Zillertal Alps

THE HIGHEST HUTS

1	Rif. Marco-e-Rosa	3597	Bernina
2	Rif. Mantova	3535	Ortler Group
3	Erzh. Johann Hut	3454	Hohe Tauern
4	Brandenburger Haus	3274	Ötztal Alps
5	Rif. Casati	3270	Ortler Group
6	Müller Hut	3148	Stubai Alps
7	Zittelhaus	3105	Hohe Tauern
8	Payer Hut	3029	Ortler Group
9	Rif. Lobbia	3020	Adamello Group
10	Similaun Hut	3017	Ötztal Alps
11	Ramol Haus	3005	Ötztal Alps
12	Oberwalder Hut	2972	Hohe Tauern
13	Hochwilde Haus	2866	Ötztal Alps
14	H. Schwaiger Haus	2802	Hohe Tauern
15	Prager Hut	2796	Hohe Tauern
16	Düsseldorf Hut	2721	Ortler Group
17	Rojacher Hut	2718	Hohe Tauern
18	Rif. Pizzini	2700	Ortler Group
19	Hintergrat Hut	2661	Ortler Group
20	Rif. dei Fiacconi	2626	Dolomite Alps
21	Marteller Hut	2610	Ortler Group
22	Lenkjöchl Hut	2589	Hohe Tauern
23	Forno Hut	2574	Bregaglia
24	Tschierva Hut	2573	Bernina
25	Eisbruggjoch Hut	2545	Zillertal Alps
26	Grialetsch Hut	2542	Albula Range
27	Weisskugel Hut	2542	Ötztal Alps
28	Martin-Busch Hut	2501	Ötztal Alps

Index